MICROSOFT POWERPOINT®

MADE EASY

2019 EDITION

Publisher and Creative Director: Nick Wells
Project Editor: Polly Prior
Art Director and Layout Design: Mike Spender
Digital Design and Production: Chris Herbert
Technical Editor: Roger Laing
Copy Editor: Daniela Nava
Proofreader: Karen Fitzpatrick
Screenshots: Chris Smith
Thanks to: Laura Bulbeck and Lydia Good

This edition first published 2019 by
FLAME TREE PUBLISHING
6 Melbray Mew
Fulham, London SW6 3NS
United Kingdom

All non-screenshot pictures are courtesy of Shutterstock and © the following photographers:
Dmitriy Shironosov 1; Diego Cervo 3; Yuri Arcurs 4, 7, 12, 218; .shock 5 t, 46; r.classen 5b, 86; Angela Waye 6t, 134;
T.W. van Urk 6b, 186; JazzBoo 41t; Tyler Boyes 73; Billion Photos 80; l i g h t p o e t 180; karam Miri 206.

ISBN 978-1-78755-725-3

Manufactured in China

1 3 5 7 9 10 8 6 4 2

MICROSOFT
POWERPOINT®
MADE EASY

2019 EDITION

CHRIS SMITH

FLAME TREE
PUBLISHING

CONTENTS

INTRODUCTION............................8

POWERPOINT BASICS.....................12

If you're unfamiliar with Microsoft PowerPoint, things can get a little intimidating. Using easy-to-digest steps, this chapter introduces this versatile presentation software and furnishes you with the knowledge needed to feel comfortable. You'll learn what PowerPoint is capable of, what you can include in a slide show and take a detailed look at the PowerPoint Window and the user interface you'll be working with en route to PowerPoint nirvana.

CREATING A PRESENTATION 46

This chapter features a comprehensive guide to creating and delivering a basic PowerPoint presentation, with step-by-step instructions on how to start a new document, add text and insert new slides. It also introduces the vast array of attractive themes and templates that Microsoft has provided to enable you to brighten up your presentation. You'll also find vital information on preparing to deliver your presentation, transferring it to the big screen and printing handouts to allow your audience to follow and make notes of their own.

IMPROVING A PRESENTATION 86

PowerPoint features a gigantic array of options for improving the look and content of a presentation. This chapter offers a detailed guide to selecting, editing and spellchecking text, while also changing the fonts, colours and style of important words. There is also plenty of advice on how to improve the look of your slide show by adding attractive animations and transitions, and creating custom slide designs.

ADDING TO A PRESENTATION 134

Now comes the fun part! This portion of the book focuses on adding meat to the bones of a PowerPoint presentation. The software allows you to add images, video and sound, as well as attractive charts, tables, shapes and SmartArt (fantastic text-based diagrams). The chapter features clear and easy-to-follow instructions for perfecting the more exciting portions of any PowerPoint document that'll keep your audience bright-eyed and bushy-tailed.

ADVANCED POWERPOINT 186

Are you ready to take things to the next level? This chapter focuses on advanced functionality like broadcasting your presentation on the web or turning your beautiful slide show into a video for the world to behold. It also illustrates how to share your presentation so colleagues can contribute, how to review changes to the document and how to create clickable slides with links to websites, other documents and more.

POWERPOINT PROJECTS 218

The final section of this book features a detailed step-by-step guide to creating fantastic PowerPoint presentations in a variety of settings: for business, for learning and for the home. Each project has been produced on either Mac or PC (although the same results can be achieved on either using the tools outlined within this book) and is accompanied by helpful screenshots so you'll see exactly how it's been done, and hopefully pick up plenty of useful tips along the way.

JARGON BUSTER 246

FURTHER READING 250

WEBSITES 251

INDEX 252

INTRODUCTION

Since its arrival on the scene in 1990, PowerPoint has developed into the world's most popular means of presenting computerized information to an audience. You'll see it in many settings: from the classroom and the office to your local pub or church. This book offers a practical and educational guide, which will quickly allow you to build up your skills while resolving the roadblocks you'll encounter on the way to producing great slide shows.

GETTING TO GRIPS WITH POWERPOINT

Although PowerPoint can appear to be quite intimidating and complex to the first-time or inexperienced user, everything is designed and laid out in a logical way, which makes it very easy to understand. This book will break down some of the boundaries and allow you to explore the full potential of the software; you'll be amazed at how straightforward everything is once the first slide is written.

Above: PowerPoint may be intimidating to the first-time user, but it is laid out logically and easy to use.

DIVE IN, DIVE OUT

This book is not meant to be read from cover to cover; frankly, we'd be worried about you if you did. It is our hope that you'll dive in and out whenever you need a helping hand to understand a particular feature or overcome a frustrating problem. If you need to learn how to add secondary paragraphs to bullet points, how to add a legend to a chart or how to make an image fit a placeholder, just look it up in the index page.

FORGET THE STIGMAS

Let's be honest: the word 'PowerPoint' doesn't really inspire positive connotations. Many of us will have sat through dull presentations, wishing to be elsewhere. However, it doesn't have to be that way; PowerPoint presentations can be as exciting, interesting and entertaining as you want to make them. All of the tools to do so are available at the click of a mouse and a few prods of the keyboard. This book will help you harness them and prove the naysayers wrong.

VERSIONS

PowerPoint is a constantly evolving platform, and each new version of the software brings changes and refinements. Features get upgraded, renamed, moved around or sometimes ditched altogether. All of this can occasionally confuse and frustrate users who are familiar with the earlier incarnations. For

Above: The updated 'Ribbon' interface is user-friendly and retains many features from previous versions, but with a sleeker look and feel.

the last decade or so, PowerPoint has relied on 'the Ribbon' interface, which relies on a series of tabs at the top of the display, offering dynamic, ever-changing options when selected. This book is largely tailored towards the new PowerPoint 2016 and PowerPoint 2019 versions, but you'll see screenshots from earlier versions littered throughout.

Above: The differences between PowerPoint for Mac and Windows will be explored throughout the book.

APPLE MAC USERS

Apple computers are as popular as ever and, thankfully for those who prefer to work with the Mac operating system rather than Windows, Microsoft makes a fully functional version of PowerPoint for both platforms. There are some subtle and not-so-subtle differences between the two pieces of software that will be explained in detail later on.

POWERPOINT ONLINE

As well as the PC and Mac versions, Microsoft offers an online version of PowerPoint that allows you to create presentations using any computer, whether the programme is installed on that machine or not. Not all features are present (for example, you can't record presentations using PowerPoint Online), but it is helpful in a pinch. This is a free version of the software anyone can use, as long as they have a Microsoft account. Most of the functionality explained here will still apply. Head to Office.com to learn more.

MOBILE APPS

PowerPoint now has powerful mobile apps for iOS (iPhone, iPad) and Android devices that can be used to display and edit presentations. While these aren't the ideal format for presentation creation, they've become a vital element of the ecosystem, especially for real-time collaboration. These apps require an Office 365 subscription to edit documents (see page 18).

Above: Chapter four of this book focuses on ways to spice up your presentation, such as inserting a chart.

SIX CHAPTERS

This book is split into six chapters and, naturally, there's a logical progression from one to the next, depending on the skill level associated with each feature of PowerPoint. Chapter one gives a quick overview for those who may be new to PowerPoint. Chapter two equips you with all of the tools necessary to create and deliver the most basic presentation to an audience. Chapter three focuses on the improvements you can make through design and text formatting tools, while in Chapter four the focus is on spicing up your presentation with a range of attractive charts, tables, videos, images and more. With some advanced tips, Chapter five will enable you to go from Padawan learner to Jedi master, while the final chapter features step-by-step case studies you can apply to creating the perfect PowerPoint presentations for work, home and school.

HOT TIPS AND SHORTCUTS

Hoping to save you a little time, we've inserted throughout the book plenty of tips to help you access some of the neat, but less obvious features within PowerPoint. Speaking of time-savers,

Microsoft has inserted a host of keyboard short cuts. These usually involve pressing two or more keys together (e.g. Control+N for a New Presentation) rather than using three or four different mouse clicks. Wherever these shortcuts are available, we'll point them out.

EASY DIGESTION

Sometimes the amount of information required to get to grips with a certain feature can be quite intimidating, so we've tried to break it down into manageable and easily digestible chunks. Rather than a gigantic Sunday roast piled on to your plate, which leaves you sluggish, demotivated and ready for a nap, think of this book as a relaxing evening picking and choosing from a tapas bar. Where necessary, we've also included a host of screenshots from the Mac, PC and Online versions to further illustrate the features described throughout.

Above: This book is easy to dip in and out of and will guide you through all the tools you need for setting up a presentation.

BUSTING THE JARGON

Although every effort has been made to keep the language and tone as user-friendly as possible, sometimes using jargon like 'placeholder' and 'AutoCorrect' is unavoidable. That's just what the features are called! Whenever you see a term or word you're unfamiliar with, head to the Glossary of Terms for an explanation (or you could use the Thesaurus tool within PowerPoint).

HELP!

Although we're confident that this book provides all of the information needed to become fluent in PowerPoint, Microsoft also includes a very useful 'Help' section within the software. Typing your query into the Help box will bring answers to any question you may have. This may be particularly useful if you're creating presentations in older versions of PowerPoint that haven't been explored in as much depth here. You can also check out the Further Reading section at the end of this book for a number of helpful websites. Microsoft's online support documentation also explains how to use all features in full. You can find it here https://support.office.com/en-gb/powerpoint.

POWERPOINT BASICS

WHAT IS POWERPOINT?

PowerPoint is a versatile piece of presentation software made by Microsoft primarily for use on desktop and laptop personal computers. These first few pages will help you to understand the very basics of what PowerPoint is, what it can do and how you can get it up and running on your computer.

Above: A presentation consists of a series of slides filled with various pieces of information, like text, pictures, charts and videos.

WHAT IS PRESENTATION SOFTWARE?

Presentation software – and, in our case, PowerPoint – is a modern combination of the traditional blackboard, whiteboard, flip chart, overhead projector slide and printed handout. It can substitute or complement any of those. A presentation consists of a series of computerized 'slides' filled with various pieces of information. The software requires a computer on which to create the presentation and a screen of some description in order to view it.

WHY USE POWERPOINT?

PowerPoint is by far the most popular software for presenting and sharing information with an audience, whether you're at home, school or work. It can be used for the most basic text-based presentations or for meticulously designed shows, which include videos,

Above: Click Start on Windows to check whether you have PowerPoint.

pictures, audio, charts, graphs and much, much more. Starting at the very beginning, we'll help you on the way to achieving both.

Do I Have It Already?

If you're coming to this book as a complete newcomer, you may be wondering how to go about obtaining PowerPoint and how to get it on to your computer. However, there's a chance you may already have it on your computer at work, school or home. If you have Microsoft Word on your computer then you probably have PowerPoint too (look for the software represented by the 'P' icon on a red folder like Word's 'W' on a blue folder within the Microsoft Office package).

Hot Tip

To check if you have PowerPoint, hit the Start button at the bottom left corner of Windows (Hit Command (⌘) + Space on Mac) and type 'PowerPoint' into the search box. If it appears in the pop-up menu then you're good to go.

PowerPoint Within Microsoft Office

Earlier versions of PowerPoint can be purchased individually, but it forms a vital component of the Microsoft Office package (or 'suite', as it's generally known). It is much more cost-effective to buy the Office suite as a whole and we can safely predict that you'll get plenty of use from the other items within the suite. Here are some of the other popular Office programs you may recognize.

Above: You may already have PowerPoint on your computer, especially if you have Microsoft Word.

-  **Word**: The world's most popular word processor, it is used to create and edit text-based documents.
- **Excel**: Software used to create spreadsheets and analyse data.
- **OneNote**: Note-taking software often used for creating to-do lists and reminders.
- **Access**: A database tool for gathering important information, such as mailing lists, in one place.
- **Outlook**: Microsoft's de facto email client used for sending and receiving email.

Above: PowerPoint for the Apple Mac is now much closer to the PC version in terms of functionality

Hot Tip

Depending on which operating system you're running, you'll be limited to which version of PowerPoint your computer can run. For example, if you're on Windows 7 or Windows 8.1 you won't be able to use Office 2019. Office.com will guide you to the correct version.

PowerPoint on the Apple Mac

Since Microsoft makes PowerPoint, a common misunderstanding is that this software is only available on Windows-based PC computers. However, Mac users need not despair. PowerPoint is also available for Mac computers. The Mac version of the software is very similar to the PC version and boasts nearly all of the same features. However, there are many differences, which are usually related to the naming of these features and the means of accessing them through the various menus, toolbars and keyboard short cuts. This book will assist Mac users in equal measure as those using PCs and when differences arise, we will point them out. However, when differences are very slight, we'll rely on your common sense to spot them and act accordingly.

PowerPoint 2019

This book will primarily focus on the latest and greatest version of the software: PowerPoint 2019 for PC and PowerPoint 2019 for Mac (generally speaking, the newer Mac versions are released a year after their Windows equivalents, but the feature sets are much the same).

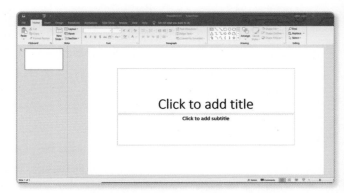

Older Versions

PowerPoint has been around in various forms for over 30 years and has constantly been updated, redesigned and improved in that time. Traditionally, Microsoft brings out at least one new version every time it operates the

Above: This book focuses on the latest versions of PowerPoint, but we'll discuss older versions throughout too.

Windows operating system. The previous version, which launched on Windows 10, was Office 2016. The previous versions, Office 2010 and Office 2013 were designed to work with Windows 7, which is still the software used by a third of all PC users worldwide.

Here are some previous versions you may have on your computer:

PowerPoint 2010 (PowerPoint 2011 for Mac)

PowerPoint 2010 for PC was more of an evolutionary version of the software, building on the revolution of PowerPoint 2007, which brought the complete change in design and user interface. It introduced the Backstage View (*see* page 35), which was a new way to manage presentation files while also adding the ability to save to the web. It also added collaboration tools, the ability to save versions of presentations, break down sections into smaller pieces and work with PowerPoint Online.

PowerPoint 2013 (PC only)

PowerPoint 2013 introduced a cleaner look, a brand new Presenter View, more options to start building a presentation with a pre-selected theme. It also added the ability to add comments to presentations when collaborating.

PowerPoint 2016

PowerPoint 2016 saw Microsoft re-organize the Ribbon menu, giving users more space to operate. It added real-time co-authoring via OneDrive cloud storage tools along with new intelligent Design Ideas. There's also new charts, shapes and transitions to spice up your presentation.

PowerPoint 2019

The latest and greatest version builds upon the previous edition while maintaining much f the same functionality of the last three versions, meaning most of our instructions will continue to apply. Specific new features include 3D models, better picture editing, the chancer to export presentations as a 4K video. You can also draw or write on a presentation with digital ink if you have a pen-friendly touchscreen PC or tablet. PowerPoint 2019 is also the first version you cannot buy as a standalone version, it only comes with the entire Office 2019 suite.

Office 365

The biggest change to Microsoft Office in recent years has been the shift towards a subscription model. Microsoft Office 365 charges a monthly, or annual fee for access to the newest and latest features, plus access to cloud-connected features that enable real-time collaboration with other users, the ability to store more documents online with 1GB of free storage.

Because Microsoft is regularly updating Office 365 with new features, it's impossible for us to keep pace with new features. If you're prompted to update the software, the accompanying documentation will inform you of new features.

Office 365 vs Office 2019

Of course, ideally speaking, you only buy any piece of software once rather than continue paying to access it year after year. That adds up over time. This is where the so-called 'on premises' versions of office come in handy.

PROS

➔ Single, one-off payment

➔ Full access to all of the Microsoft Office apps on your PC or Mac

➔ Limited access to online sharing

CONS

➔ No new feature updates after purchase

➔ Less regular security updates

➔ Limited access to mobile applications

➔ No access to online technical support

➔ No additional online storage.

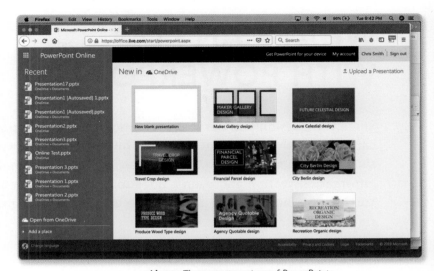

Above: The newest versions of PowerPoint include powerful online features that enable you to collaborate online in real time

Hot Tip

If you're running Windows 10 on your PC you'll get Office 365 with the newest features constantly being updated. If you're on Windows 7 or Windows 8.1, Office 365 comes with Office 2016 features.

Using This Book with Older Versions of PowerPoint

This book is largely based around the tools within PowerPoint 2019 for PC and Mac. However, if you're working with any of the versions listed above, it'll still be helpful because a large proportion of the functionality is available in the earlier versions – just accessible in slightly different ways.

WHAT CAN I DO WITH POWERPOINT?

Since the possibilities are endless, a more fitting question might be: 'What can't I do with PowerPoint?' You can build a college presentation, family slide show, business pitch, fitness plan, karaoke lyric sheet, an interactive information station and even a question slide show for the local pub quiz. You may be familiar with some of the uses we'll highlight, but others may surprise you.

WHERE POWERPOINT IS USED

Unless you're a newcomer to planet Earth, you will probably have been exposed to a PowerPoint presentation in one or more of their many forms.

In the Office

The occasional misuse or overuse of PowerPoint in the workplace has earned it a reputation as an effective cure for insomnia, but it really doesn't have to be that way. With a little help from these pages, you'll be able to pull off the following with engaging panache.

- **Sales reports:** For more perspective on improved figures, you can create a presentation loaded with attractive visual charts.

- **Pitching an idea:** If you've had a brainwave then a slide show can better illustrate your 'Eureka!' moment.

- **Training employees:** PowerPoint shows can help newcomers to settle in while learning more about their new position and company.

➔ **Job interview**: As application rates continue to rise, everyone's looking for an edge and a head-turning slideshow could be yours.

In the Classroom

This software has been a time-saving godsend for both teachers and students looking for an interesting way to present their lectures and work.

Above: With a little help from these pages, you'll be able to pull off using PowerPoint in the office with panache.

➔ **Lectures**: Accompanied by a printed handout (*see* page 64) on which students can make their own notes, these presentations are a great way to deliver information in easy-to-digest portions.

➔ **Homework/Coursework**: PowerPoint makes it easy to remember your key talking points, while helping you to move at a lively pace that keeps things interesting for your classmates and tutors.

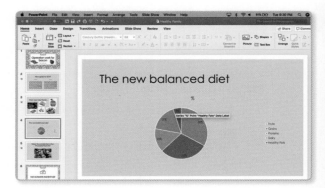

Above: A PowerPoint presentation at home can be great for sharing special memories, organizing a trip with the help of maps and videos or even planning a family diet!

At Home

A PowerPoint presentation in the home can be a great tool to rally the troops for a trip or to present special memories.

➔ **Photo albums**: PowerPoint features a number of tools for easily crafting annotated photo albums complete with video, a soundtrack and more.

Planning a trip: If you're exploring the great outdoors, you can pack a presentation with maps, videos and information about your destination.

Family budgeting/dieting: Time for a bit of belt tightening (literally and figuratively) at home? Here's how you sell it to the rest of the clan.

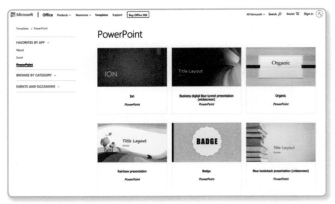

Above: Office.com templates offer a number of less familiar PowerPoint uses such as for a CV, invitation, calendar or family tree.

Office Online templates

We'll explain templates in greater detail within Chapter two (*see* page 53) but their presence merits a mention here, as easily accessible, user designed templates enable us to use PowerPoint in a number of less familiar ways. They deliver a much wider range of templates than the stock options. You can find them by searching for templates or by heading to https://templates.office.com.

Beyond the Holy Trinity

This versatile software can also be put to good use in other situations.

Information posts: Museums and galleries are using PowerPoint to create interactive stations where visitors can learn more about exhibits, watch video, listen to audio or answer trivia.

Lyrics sheets: If you co-ordinate a choir or are responsible for furnishing your parishioners with hymn lyrics, you can easily create and project song sheets.

Resumés and Cover letters: Give your résumé a well-earned refresh.

➔ **Birthday invitation**: Create an invitation which would make your five-year-old proud.

➔ **Calendar**: Easy-to-edit calendars, and attractive financial and academic year planners.

➔ **Family Tree**: Charting and presenting your family history.

➔ **Labels**: Ideal for large gatherings.

THE ROAD TO A SUCCESSFUL POWERPOINT SHOW

In order to whet your appetite for what lies ahead, we thought of a way to compare a PowerPoint presentation to a delicious meal. A hamburger (or in our case, text) is always nice, but it's always better if you add cheese (pictures), bacon (video), mushrooms (pie charts) and grilled onions (audio).

SLIDES

Within a PowerPoint presentation, the different pages are called 'slides'. To continue with our hamburger analogy, slides are the bread rolls on which to place all of those yummy fillings: the text, audio, video, etc. As you move from slide to slide, your presentation will progress in much the same way that an old-fashioned carousel slide projector moves through photographs.

Hot Tip

Keep it simple. Depending on your purposes, simply adding text is enough to create an adequate presentation... but where's the fun in that?

Within PowerPoint there's an array of slide designs you can choose from to suit your presentation, and once you've mastered the basics, you can get fancy and take a stab at designing your own.

Text

The easiest way to get started with PowerPoint is to create a presentation filled only with words, which is where Chapter two (*see* page 48) comes in handy. You can type directly into a pre-made text box called a content placeholder (*see* page 59) using your PC's or laptop's keyboard, just as you would if you were writing a Microsoft Word document. However, bullet points or lists are often used in presentations to introduce talking points that are then explained more in-depth.

Above: It's so simple to embellish your presentation with your own photos or striking images from the internet!

Pictures

It's now easier than ever to spice up your presentation with images from your own photo library or from across the web. There's also an array of stock photos available from the ClipArt library to add a little more colour to your show.

Video

Videos shot on your own camera or even on your mobile phone can be seamlessly added to your show. If you've spotted an inspirational video you would like to include (using websites such as YouTube, for example) we will show you how.

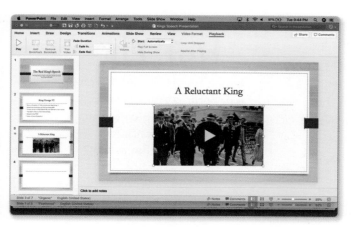

Above: It's simple to add videos to your show that you've shot using your camera or mobile phone, or from your PC or Mac, or even from the internet.

Charts

With the help of a massive array of colourful and attractive styles, PowerPoint allows you to convert figures into easy-on-the-eye bar charts, pie charts, scatter graphs, line graphs, and so on.

Tables

Tables can fulfil the need to present data, such as sales figures, in a well-organized manner. It is much easier than you think to add that series of columns and rows to your slideshow and, with a host of design options, the result will look even better than you may have anticipated.

SmartArt

SmartArt allows you to convert text and data into flow charts or diagrams. These can help to get a message across in a more visual manner than text-based bullet points would allow.

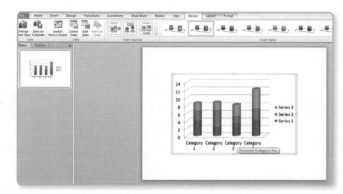

Above: There is a huge range of colourful and attractive styles to make your figures come to life in an appealing array of charts.

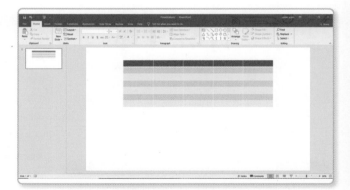

Above: Tables are a solid and versatile way to present information. It is simple to add columns and rows and the design options will make your data easy on the eye.

OLDER VERSIONS? If you're using PowerPoint 2003, primitive versions of SmartArt can be added to presentations; they're called Diagrams.

Hot Tip

Use a SmartArt chart instead of a bullet point list when presenting step-by-step information.

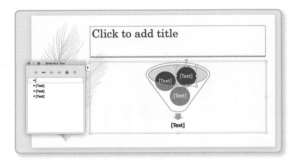

Above: Features such as SmartArt can help to bring information to life, making a welcome change from basic bullet point presenting techniques.

Hot Tip

Use animations when creating a quiz; there's no point in the answer appearing at the same time as the question.

Above: You can add and customize your own shapes and boxes for each new slide.

Audio

It's easy to add a soundtrack to a presentation by selecting songs or sounds from your computer that will play at your command when you're delivering the information to the audience. A relevant audio clip can be a great way to keep viewers engaged.

Transitions

A stylish touch to keep everything flowing smoothly, transitions control how the slide show progresses from one slide to the next. You can have fades, flashes, wipes and dissolves, much like you'd see between cuts in a movie scene.

Animations

Like transitions, animations can also add a little icing to the cake by managing how objects appear within your slides; pictures can fly into the screen and then spin off with the click of your mouse. Animations are very important when controlling the order in which information appears.

Shapes and Drawing

Shapes, like text and picture boxes, often appear when adding new slides to a presentation. However, you can add your own shapes and boxes (rectangles, circles, etc.) when designing slides. You can also draw shapes like arrows and equation signs to help illustrate your point, and the line tool can also help you to draw freehand.

MOVING AROUND THE POWERPOINT WINDOW

Now that we're more acquainted with what PowerPoint is, what it is capable of and the ingredients available to us when creating a tasty slideshow, we're ready to take a look around the PowerPoint Window.

STARTING POWERPOINT ON A PC

Firstly, you'll need to open the software. This will vary slightly depending on which version of Windows you're using. On Windows 10, click Start (the Windows icon in the bottom-left corner), begin typing 'PowerPoint' in the search box just above and the PowerPoint icon (a document with an orange P) will appear. Move your mouse to hover over the icon and click.

Alternatively, click Start, select All Apps and scroll through the alphabetical list on the left and select PowerPoint. It may also appear under a Microsoft Office menu.

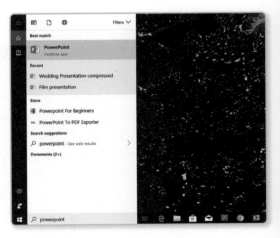

Hot Tip

Once PowerPoint is open, right-click on the icon in the Windows taskbar (at the bottom of the screen) and select 'Pin this program to taskbar' to ensure it stays there for easy access even when the program is closed.

Above: It is simple to open PowerPoint from the start menu. From here you can choose to pin the programme to your taskbar or create a shortcut.

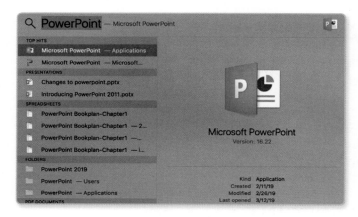

Above: On a Mac you can find PowerPoint in the Finder folder, in the dock, or by searching with the Spotlight search bar (shown above).

STARTING POWERPOINT ON A MAC

Once you've installed Microsoft Office on your Mac it'll automatically appear in the Applications folder. You can find it by hitting the Finder icon (the two faces) and browsing to Applications. Double click PowerPoint to open.

➔ Another way is to press and hold one of the Command buttons on the keyboard they're either side of the space bar) and then hit Space. This brings up the Spotlight search bar. Type 'PowerPoint' and click when it pops up in the window.

THE POWERPOINT WINDOW

Once you've opened the software, you'll have to make your first choice. You will be presented with a gallery of templates, which you can choose a number of pre-set themes for your PowerPoint presentation. On the left hand side, you'll also see the opportunity to open Recent presentations, Shared presentations (Office 365 feature) and Open all of the others.

Hot Tip

To ensure that the PowerPoint program stays within the dock, right-click (Control+Click), hover over 'Options' and hit 'Keep in Dock'.

Right now, we'll select Blank Presentation, which brings you to the main workspace. Absolutely everything you need to do within PowerPoint can be controlled or achieved from within this screen. The screenshot below represents what you'll see when you first open PowerPoint.

Current Slide

In the centre of the screen you'll see the Current Slide view, which represents, as the name suggests, what appears on the slide you're currently working on. When you open PowerPoint, there'll be only a single Title slide (as you can see to the right).

Slide View

Within the left column of the window sits the Slide View. This is where each of your slides will appear in a thumbnail view as you are working on your project, and the Current Slide is automatically highlighted in this section. Using the Slide tab, you'll see mini representations of your slides, complete with pictures and charts. Clicking Outline will make it easier to control the text, as it shows a more detailed view of the titles, subtitles and words that appear on the slide.

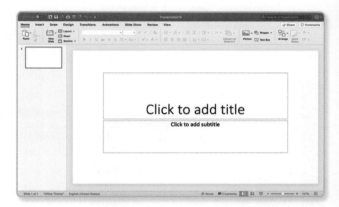

Above: This is what you will see when you first open PowerPoint.

The Ribbon

The Ribbon interface underpins the entire PowerPoint experience. Think of the Ribbon as our Mission Control centre. You'll see tabs representing Home, Insert, Design, Transitions, etc. Clicking on these tabs will dynamically change the options available to you within the interface. For example, the Home tab features options such as adding new slides, selecting slide layouts, selecting text fonts and adding

Above: The different tabs and the options within them allow you to seamlessly work through the different stages of your presentation.

> # Hot Tip
> Play around with the Ribbon by selecting the various tabs and familiarize yourself with the options available within each.

shapes. If you then hit 'Insert' next door, the Ribbon changes completely and allows you to choose charts, pictures, clip art, and so on. On the Mac version of PowerPoint, the Ribbon contains slightly different features (*see* page 34).

The File Tab and the Backstage View (PC Only)

The first tab within the Ribbon merits a little more explanation, as it differs so greatly from the others. Clicking File on a PC will bring up the 'Backstage View', which is named as such because it allows you to control the behind the scenes and, some might say, less glamorous aspects of the PowerPoint presentation. From here you can, among other things, save your presentation, send it to print and open older ones. There's more about the File tab, which arrived with PowerPoint 2010 and is a PC-only feature, within the Navigating, Opening, Saving, Closing section on page 35.

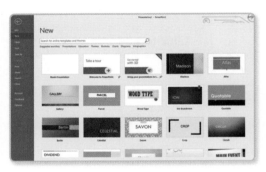

Above: File tab differs from the others and presents you with behind the scenes decisions, such as saving and printing, rather than layout and design options.

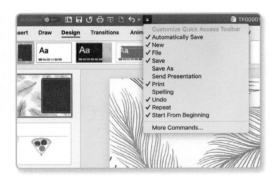

Above: The Quick Access Toolbar allows you to customize the tools and commands that you use most frequently.

Quick Access Toolbar

The Quick Access Toolbar (QAT), as the name suggests, allows faster access to your favourite tools and commands, and it first appeared within PowerPoint 2007 with the Ribbon interface. You can add more options, but the default tools are: Save, Undo, Redo and Print. You can also turn the AutoSave setting on and off here.

Customizing the QAT

In order to add items to the QAT like Save As, Star, New Presentation, etc, click the small arrow positioned to the right of the items currently residing in the toolbar to access the drop down menu seen in the screenshot on the right. Tick the item you want to add to the QAT. The More Commands option helps you add further commands.

Notes Tab

At the bottom of the PowerPoint Window you'll see a thin text box beneath the current slide containing holding text reading 'Click to add notes'. Click within this box to enter the notes pane. Here you can type notes related to each of the slides. These won't appear in your presentation but can serve as helpful reminders when designing and presenting your slide show.

Status Bar

Beneath the Notes pane and within the PowerPoint Window's border, the Status Bar offers a few key details regarding your presentation. Different versions of PowerPoint feature slightly different versions. They are, from left to right, listed below.

- **Indicator**: Explains which slide you're working within.
- **Theme**: Indicates which theme is currently in use.
- **Spellchecker**: A tick or a cross within this button indicates whether there are spelling errors that need attention (PC only).
- **Notes**: Click this to hide and show notes you've made on each slide.
- **Viewing options**: Clicking each of these small boxes changes how your presentation appears on the screen. The default is Normal View but you can also select Slide Sorter, which makes it easy to rearrange the order of your slides, or Reading View, which maximizes the size of the slide to fill the PowerPoint Window. The latter is great for practising your presentation. The final option is Slide Show view, which you should use when you're ready to showcase your work.

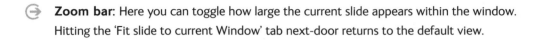

Zoom bar: Here you can toggle how large the current slide appears within the window. Hitting the 'Fit slide to current Window' tab next-door returns to the default view.

Scroll Bars

These are displayed when the window contains more content than can be viewed on the screen; they are used to navigate around the presentation. They appear to the right of your panes (i.e. Current Slide, Slide View, Notes) but when you've zoomed in on a slide, a horizontal slide bar will appear.

A CLOSER LOOK AT THE RIBBON

As we've mentioned, the Ribbon is the key to controlling PowerPoint and is a much more user-friendly and efficient way of accessing key features of the program. To move between the tabs, you can hover over the title with your cursor and click to reveal the new design, formatting and viewing tools that'll open up to the right of the window. Here's a quick look at what you can do within each tab, but there's more on this in chapter two and beyond (*see* page 48).

Hot Tip

If you're working with multiple presentations, you can showcase them on the same screen. View 'Arrange All'. On the PowerPoint 2019 for Mac, hit Window in the Menu Bar to access the same option.

Home: Add new slides, copy, cut and paste content; change font, alignment, style and size of text and draw shapes.

Insert: An easy way to add pictures, videos, audio, text boxes, screenshots shapes, charts, tablets, ClipArt, WordArt, as well as headers and footers, dates, symbols, equations and more.

Draw: New to PowerPoint, the Draw tab lets you annotate slides with freehand pen tools and your trackpad. This feature works best with touchscreens and electronic pens/styluses.

Design: Adjust the project's theme, colour scheme, font group, theme effects and the style of slide backgrounds. You can also adjust the page set-up and slide orientation.

Transitions: Control how the slide show progresses (Fade, Push, Wipe, etc.) and adjust the direction and speed at which a transition moves.

Animations: Drop animations and effects that control how items arrive in and leave the slides (i.e. Fly In, Fade In). You can control their duration and order.

Slide Show: Play your presentation, rehearse its timings and prepare it for broadcasting online.

Review: Before you complete your show, you can check spelling, research facts, translate into new languages and add comments.

View: Change how your presentation appears on screen, open Master views and adjust colours.

Additional Tabs

Invariably, new tabs will appear within the Ribbon as you work with PowerPoint; for example, if you insert a picture into a slide a Picture Format tab will appear at the end of the Ribbon. We'll explain these as we come to them.

The Ribbon on the Apple Mac

Mac users will see a slightly different set of Ribbon tabs. For starters, the File tab still resides within the familiar Apple menu bar rather than in the Ribbon. There are some other slight differences, but mostly these differences pertain to slightly different names of features. We'll explain these as we go along.

Above: The Home tab allows you to access slide and formatting features effortlessly.

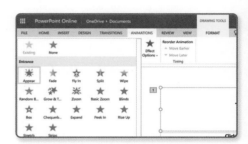

Above: The Animations tab (shown in PowerPoint Online) allows you to control how information arrives on your slide.

Above: The Ribbon tab options for Mac differ slightly from those for a PC.

NAVIGATING, OPENING, SAVING AND CLOSING

Now that we're familiar with our surroundings within the PowerPoint Window and have untangled the Ribbon user interface, let's try our hand at navigating around the PowerPoint software and exploring some basic navigational and housekeeping functionality before we create our first presentation.

THE CURSOR

When you wave your mouse around within the PowerPoint Window, a small arrow moves around with you. Stopping and hovering over an icon, menu or feature allows you to click and select that item. The arrow appears most of the time when navigating around PowerPoint but, within the software, the cursor takes different forms depending on what you're doing.

Arrow: Used for selecting items, menus and features.

'I' cursor: Displayed when working within text or tables.

Up/down arrow: Appears when extending a text box/shape vertically.

Left/right arrow: Appears when extending a text box/shape horizontally.

Up/Down/Left/Right arrow: Appears when moving a box/shape/item.

Scrolling

In order to move up and down (or left to right) within a scroll bar (*see* page 33), use your mouse to click the arrows at each end. For more precision you can grab the scroll bar with your mouse or trackpad (click and hold the left button) and move it up/down/left/right. If you're using a touchscreen PC you can use your fingers!

THE BACKSTAGE VIEW

If the Ribbon represents the functioning organs of the PowerPoint software, the Backstage View is the backbone (PC only). Within the Backstage View in PowerPoint 2010 you can find all of the key information about your current presentation, while a tab on the left-hand side gives you access to a host of essential options. Click the File tab on the Ribbon to see the Backstage View.

Info Screen

The Info section is at the top of the File tag. From there you'll be able to perform some of the more advanced functions from the dropdown menus, which we'll tackle later but are listed here for reference.

⊖ **Permissions/Protect Presentations**: Add a password to stop others accessing or editing the presentation and mark it as complete so collaborators know not to change it.

⊖ **Prepare for sharing/Inspect presentations**: Inspect the document to ensure there's no unwanted personal information, make it disability friendly and check that it'll work with previous versions of PowerPoint.

⊖ **Properties:**
In the panel to the right of the screen you can, among other things, add authors, and see file sizes, last saved date and last modified date.

Right: The Info section in Backstage View is automatically highlighted when you enter the File tab.

Other Backstage View Features

There's plenty more to do backstage, as illustrated by the tabs on the left-hand side of the screen. In order to access them, click the relevant tab and you'll see new options present themselves to the right of the screen.

⊙ **New:** When you click this tab, you'll be presented with a newly populated menu offering you the chance to start a new presentation from a host of template options (*see* page 51).

⊙ **Open:** Open an existing PowerPoint presentation.

⊙ **Save/Save As:** Ensure the latest version of your presentation is stored securely. For Save As, save a newer version of your presentation, but under a different file name. You can also choose a location to save it, like OneDrive and your PC.

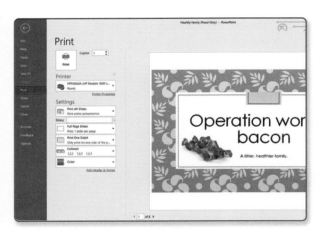

⊙ **Print:** Access print options, such as how many copies to print, which printer, how many slides per page, colours and more.

⊙ **Close:** Close the Presentation (if you haven't saved it yet, you'll be prompted to) but not the PowerPoint program.

⊙ **Share:** Here you can choose a number of options to share your in progress or completed presentation with colleagues.

Above: When you attempt to print your PowerPoint presentation you'll have a wide range of customization options.

⊙ **Options:** General and extensive PowerPoint options that will allow you to customize the Ribbon and the Quick Access Toolbar among other things.

SAVING A PRESENTATION

Losing your work to a computer crash, breakage, theft or some other act of God is forgivable; however, losing weeks of meticulously crafted PowerPoint perfection through forgetting to save is not. There are several ways to ensure that, by regularly saving your work, you won't join the scores of unfortunate souls.

➜ Click the Save icon (the floppy disc) in the Quick Access Toolbar.

➜ Use a 'keyboard shortcut' by holding down the Control key and pressing the S key.

Keyboard shortcuts more often than not involve holding the Control key and pressing another – or simply pressing both at the same time. In this case it's Control+S (or Command+S on the Apple Mac).

➜ Hit the File tab and click Save.

If this is the first time you're saving your work you'll be presented with a pop-up dialogue box where you'll be asked to give your project a name and a location in which to save it. Type in the name you've chosen over the highlighted text that'll say 'Presentation 1' and click the OK box.

Saving a New Version of Your Presentation

If you want to save a new version of your slide show but keep the older one (this is useful if you're tailoring a similar presentation for

Hot Tip

In order to exit the File tab, click it again or hit one of the other tabs in the Ribbon.

Above: When a file is saved for the first time, the Save As dialogue box will allow you to name your file and choose where to save it.

different audiences), you can use the Save As functionality. This is less important with newer versions of PowerPoint that enable you to access different versions of your presentation.

→   Control+Shift+SS (Command+Shift+S on the Apple Mac).

→   Click File and select Save As.

You'll again be greeted with a pop-up window where you'll need to give your new presentation a slightly different name, enter it into the dialogue box and then press Save.

POWERPOINT FILE EXTENSIONS

For the most part, this is something you will not need to worry about. However, when you save your presentation, you can add different file extensions to ensure your project will work onolder versions of the software or on machines where PowerPoint is not installed.

Types of File Extension

A file extension is the lettering that appears after the dot when saving a file (for example, TestPresentation.pptx). When you first save your file, you'll see a drop-down menu that reads 'Save as type' (called Format on Macs) and here are some of the options to consider at this stage.

Hot Tip

If you want to edit your presentation on multiple machines, choose to save your presentation to OneDrive. It can then be downloaded to another computer.

Hot Tip

PowerPoint also has a version management tool that allows you to access Versions of a presentation at various save states. Hit File > Info > Version History on PC.

Hot Tip

Give your project a logical name you'll remember and save it to a familiar destination such as your Documents folder. When you first save your presentation, that's where PowerPoint will want to put it. Let it do you a favour.

⊕ **PowerPoint Presentation (.pptx):** This is the default save setting. Files will work on computers with PowerPoint 2010 and PowerPoint 2007 but will not open on computers running earlier versions of PowerPoint, such as PowerPoint 2003.

⊕ **PowerPoint Presentation (.ppt):** Allows the presentation to open in any version of PowerPoint, old or new.

⊕ **PDF (.pdf):** This will allow the presentation to be displayed even if the computer you're using does not have PowerPoint. However, it cannot be edited this way.

⊕ **XPS (.xps):** Similar to the above but XPS was developed by Microsoft (PC only), whereas PDF was developed by Adobe.

Saving to the Cloud

This enables the presentation to live online, in the cloud. It means you can access presentations when you're away from your own computer, share them with others and safeguard them in the event that your computer is lost, stolen or broken. Microsoft's cloud solution is called OneDrive.

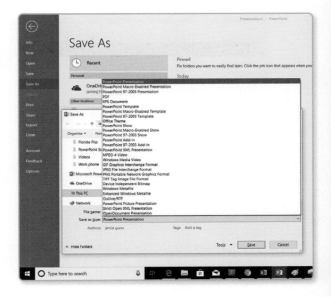

Above: There are various types of file extension you can choose, depending on your needs.

Above: On a PC hit File > Save As > OneDrive to save a file to OneDrive.

Above: You can save multiple documents on OneDrive to be accessed when away from your own computer.

Accessing OneDrive

In order to save a document to OneDrive, you'll to have a free online account with Microsoft. This can be a Hotmail email account, Outlook.com account, a Windows Live account, Xbox Live, etc. The chances are, if you've spent any time on the internet over the years, you have at least one of these (to sign up and get visit Office.com).

➔ **To save to OneDrive on a PC**: hit File > Save As > OneDrive.

➔ **To save to OneDrive on a Mac**: hit File > Save As > select OneDrive from the Dialogue box and log in.

OPENING A PRESENTATION

When you open the software you'll be presented with the blank PowerPoint Window. In order to access presentations you've previously worked on, choose one of the following options and then click on the file name of your choice to recommence work on that slide show.

➔ Use the keyboard shortcut Control+O (Command+O on the Mac).

➔ Click the File tab and select Open.

➔ Click the File tab and hit Recent (hit File then Open Recent on the Mac).

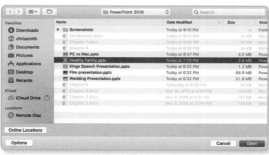

Above: From the Open dialogue box, documents which have already been started can be accessed and opened.

Open your Documents folder (or wherever you've stored your presentation) and double-click the relevant file. This will open PowerPoint with your chosen project.

Hot Tip

Mac users take note: whenever you see a keyboard shortcut that asks you to press Control+ another key, for you this means pressing Command (the two keys either side of the space bar) + another key.

CHANGING THE SIZE OF THE POWERPOINT WINDOW

Viewing other items on your computer can be made a little easier by minimizing or reducing the size of your PowerPoint Window. This can be achieved by using the tools in the top right corner of the window (or the left for Mac users).

Minimize: Clicking the 'minus' icon will keep your presentation open but send it to the taskbar

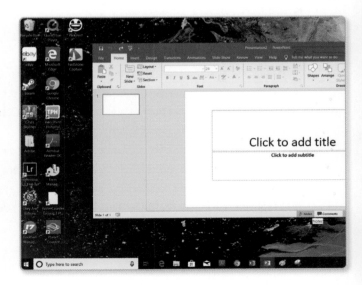

Above: The PowerPoint Window can be restored down from full screen to around half the screen size.

at the bottom of the screen (into the dock on Mac). To restore it, click the PowerPoint icon within the taskbar.

Restore Down (PC only): Clicking the two-box icon will reduce the size of the PowerPoint Window to around half of your screen size.

Maximize: Hitting the single square box icon (which appears when the window is restored down) will make PowerPoint appear in full screen view.

Full Screen (Mac): Hitting the green dot will give PowerPoint your undivided attention.

CLOSING POWERPOINT

After a lengthy session of hard work crafting your PowerPoint presentation, it can be satisfying to close everything down and put your feet up or, in many cases, start work on something else. Here's how.

1. Click the X in the top right corner to close the current presentation. If you only have one presentation open, this will close the PowerPoint program.
2. Similarly, use the keyboard shortcut Control+W (Command+W on Mac) to close the presentation you're working on.
3. Click the File tab and then Close on the left-hand side to close the current project.
4. Click the File tab and then Exit to close the program (File and then Quit PowerPoint on the Mac; the Command+Q short cut also works here).
5. Right-click the icon in the taskbar (dock on a Mac) and hit 'Close window' (Quit).

Accidental Closing and AutoSave

If you have unsaved changes to your presentation, PowerPoint will also issue a pop-up warning and give you the opportunity to save. However, sometimes software and computers can crash, but don't worry: you won't lose everything if AutoSave is enabled. PowerPoint automatically background saves your presentation every 10 minutes and will keep the last AutoSaved version if the program ever closes without saving. In order to access the AutoSave settings and alter how often your work is backed up, hit File > Options > Save (PowerPoint menu > Preferences > Save, on the Mac).

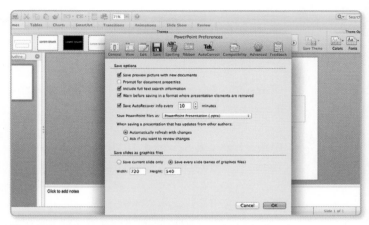

Above: The settings of the AutoSave function can be easily altered, such as how often documents are backed up.

AutoSave and Office 365

One of the benefits of an Office 365 subscription is the constant AutoSave functionality. You'll see the tool in the QAT and switching it on will ensure any changes are continually saved. If you're saving the document to OneDrive they will be synced online too.

OLDER VERSIONS? If you're using PowerPoint 2003, you can access the AutoSave settings by selecting Tools > Options. In PowerPoint 2007 hit Office Button and then PowerPoint options.

OBTAINING POWERPOINT

The fact that you're already reading this book has led us to the assumption that you've already got PowerPoint on your PC, but if you haven't, there are a number of ways to get it.

⊖ **Download the software online:** To get the software right now, without leaving your keyboard, point your web browser (Internet Explorer, Google Chrome or Firefox) to Office.com/buy. You can download the software and install directly to your PC or Mac. Microsoft presents you with three options when you do.

➔ **Office 365 Home**: This gives access to the Office 365 subscription platform, meaning all of the features explained on page 18). It costs $99.99 a year or $9.99 a month and offers access for up to 6 users.

➔ **Office 365 Personal**: As above, but for a single user. It costs $69.99 a year, but with no monthly payment option.

➔ **Office Home & Student 2019**: A one off purchase for $149 a year. There's no Office 365 features available. It can only be installed on one PC or Mac.

➔ **Free trials**: If you want to try before you buy, or just use PowerPoint for a limited amount of time, Microsoft offers a 30-day trial of the entire Office 365 package that allows you to download and use the software. You'll see these options when you select which version to buy. One the trial is over, you'll need to subscriber to Office 365 if you wish to keep using.

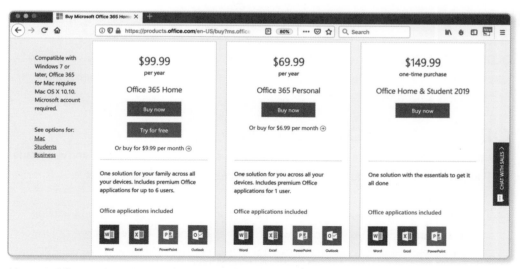

Above: At Office.com/buy a free trial of Microsoft Office 365 is available

Download and installing PowerPoint

Once you've selected which version of Office you wish to buy, you'll be able to download the software and install it. It's quite a large file so may take a while depending on how fast your internet connection is. Once the download is complete, you'll be able to install and begin using PowerPoint. If you're using Office 365 you'll be asked to log in to the software with your Microsoft account.

Mobile apps

If you're an Office 365 subscriber you'll get access to the standalone PowerPoint app for iPhone, iPad and Android. That means you can view, edit, create and stare documents. The free version only provides the ability to view documents from OneDrive or others that have been shared with you.

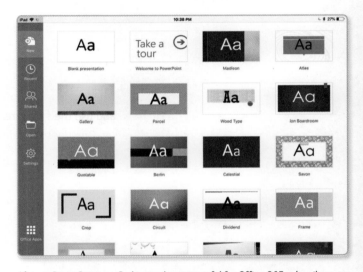

Above: PowerPoint on iPad is much more useful for Office 365 subscribers

- **iPhone or iPad**: Go to App Store on your iOS device, search for PowerPoint. Click 'Get' and authenticate the download. Once you've opened the app, you can sign into view, edit and create documents.

- **Android**: Tap the Play Store icon and Search for PowerPoint. Download the app and follow the instructions above.

Hot Tip

If you wish to gift Microsoft Office, your local electronics store will sell Product Keys for Microsoft Office as a gift card. Recipients can follow a link, download the software and enter the product key to begin using.

CREATING A PRESENTATION

FROM START TO FINISH AND EVERYTHING IN BETWEEN

In this chapter we'll give you all of the information necessary to create and present a basic, text-based PowerPoint presentation. You'll learn how to edit and add slides, while employing themes and templates that will add style to your slide show. We'll also explain how to print handouts for your audience and illustrate the different ways to present your creation.

STARTING A NEW PRESENTATION

Once you've opened the PowerPoint software on your PC or Mac (*see* page 27), you will automatically be greeted with the ability to choose your course. You'll see a number of colourful templates, but we're going to start with the most basic. If this isn't your first PowerPoint rodeo, the software will open up existing presentations. To start a brand-new one, hit the shortcut Control+N or Command+N for Mac users.

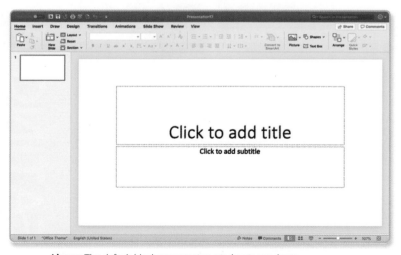

Above: The default blank presentation window is very basic.

The Blank Presentation PowerPoint Window

This default setting, with which we will be working initially, features the simple Office theme, which has no design bells or whistles. It contains a single Title Slide, which invites a title and a subtitle for your presentation with the message 'Click to add text'.

CONFIGURING PAGE SET-UP AND SLIDE ORIENTATION

After all of this build-up, you must certainly be eager to start filling those text boxes and begin adding slides. However, there are a couple of housekeeping matters to take care of, such as page set-up and orientation of slides. Configuring these early on is important, as they can affect the look and feel of your slides later on when you've already added content. Hit the Design tab in the Ribbon. In the 'Customize' section to the right, there's Slide Size option.

Hot Tip

On PC you'll see each element of a Ribbon tab identified by different sections like 'Customize' in the Design tab. Mac users don't have these named, so we'll point you towards the right area.

Hot Tip

Within the Page Set-up pop-up, you can also select whether Notes and Handouts will be printed in Portrait or Landscape.

Slide Orientation

You can change the layout of your slides from the default Landscape view to Portrait. Most commonly, PowerPoint presentations are Landscape, but if you plan to create letter-headed paper, for example, you'll need to go Portrait. In order to carry out this change, select the Page Set-up drop down menu.

Slide Sizes and Aspect ratio

When adjusting the size of your slide, you need to take into account where you'll be presenting your slide show. When you hit the Slide Size button, the default setting shows slides at an aspect ratio of Widescreen 16:9 akin to modern laptop screens, but you can also change to 4:3

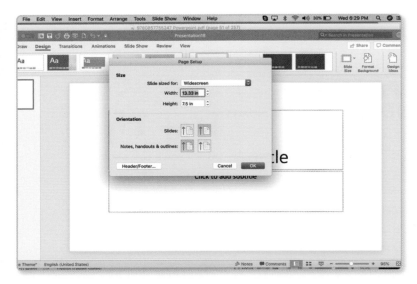

(devices like tablet). This is important for displaying the presentation correctly on screen. It's better to decide on this setting at the beginning than at the end, because it affects the way content is displayed too.

Left: Slides are automatically set up at a 4:3 aspect ratio, but the ratio can be changed (as seen here on a Mac).

You can also manually adjust the width and height of slides, but there's no need for us to concern ourselves with this if you're going to get super fancy. In order to adjust the aspect ratio of slides, select Page Set-up and choose from the drop-down 'Slides sized for' menu.

Above: Slides are automatically set up at a 4:3 aspect ratio, but the ratio can be changed (as seen here on a PC).

THEMES AND TEMPLATES

Themes and templates are attractive design pre-sets that allow you to add a colourful flavour to your presentation. They're extremely easy to insert and there are loads to choose from to suit the tone and purpose of your slide show perfectly.

WHAT ARE THEMES?

Think of PowerPoint themes as if you were completely redecorating your home. Not every room is going to be the same, but even the most amateur interior decorator would want there to be some sort of style consistency throughout the house. Without a PowerPoint

Above: PowerPoint themes, such as the Berlin theme seen here, add style consistency to the slides.

Theme, you're simply placing the furniture (words, pictures, video, etc.) in white-painted rooms without coloured paint, wallpaper, borders or that stuff that makes an empty house your home.

WHAT'S IN A THEME?

There are a number of elements that combine to comprise a theme in PowerPoint. Most of them are there to make life easier for the user and to ensure that the presentation maintains a universally attractive and co-ordinated form. Chapter three is loaded with information on how to customize your theme with the following.

Hot Tip

Hovering over the various themes with the cursor automatically offers a view of how your presentation will look with that theme, helping you to decide which one is most suitable.

➡ **Colours:** Each theme has a colour scheme, which helpfully brings together a series of shades that work well together. However, you can select from a number of different colour schemes that also bring together co-ordinated colours.

➡ **Fonts:** Just like with colours, there are certain fonts that work well together. Themes combine them, with one font for headings and another complementary font for content text.

➡ **Slide layouts:** Within PowerPoint there are a number of pre-set slide layouts that you can select when adding new slides (*see* page 61). For example, there are Title slides, Title and Content slides (which allow you to type a title and then add a content item below), and so on. Each theme presents these layouts in a slightly different way.

➡ **Background styles:** As well as the above, each theme boasts its own background style that sits behind all of the content. This menu contains available colours and gradient shading for your slides, which will help to avoid nasty colour clashes.

HOW TO SELECT A THEME

As referenced earlier, PowerPoint will give you the opportunity to select a theme from a Template when starting a new presentation. However, from your Blank Presentation Window you can also choose a theme before, during and after adding content to your slides. Select the Design tab from the Ribbon and a number of colourful suggestions will present themselves as thumbnail slides.

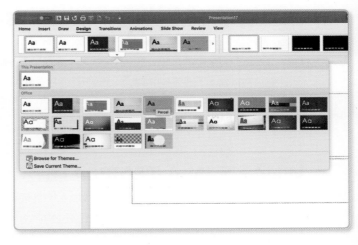

Above: A variety of themes, presented as thumbnails, are available to view.

WHAT ARE TEMPLATES?

Earlier in this chapter, we compared the use of themes in PowerPoint to decorating your house. Templates are very similar and many of the same options are present as Themes, but additional templates are also designed for a specific purpose and with greater customization like placeholder text, transitions and animations. For example, see the Training New Employees template in slide sorter view in the screenshot (right).

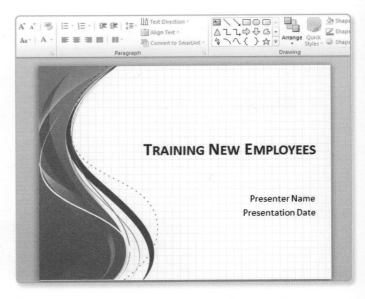

Above: Templates are an easy way to create attractive presentations.

Finding the right template

If you want a template for a specific purpose, chances are there's a template available for it. The options you'll displayed on the New From Templates screen are effectively Themes. However, you can begin typing in the search car for key terms that will bring up templates. The PC version of the software suggests terms like business, education, industry, personal and nature The Sports Presentation to the right was found just by typing 'sport'.

WHAT'S IN A TEMPLATE?

Like the Themes, starting a presentation from a Template presents a look and feel for your presentation that remains consistent. However, while a Theme starts with a single slide you can add to, a Template offers an entire series of pre-designed slides in various styles. You're able to customize these, add or delete slides too. Another difference from Themes is that all transitions and effects are also added to the presentation (*see* page 115).

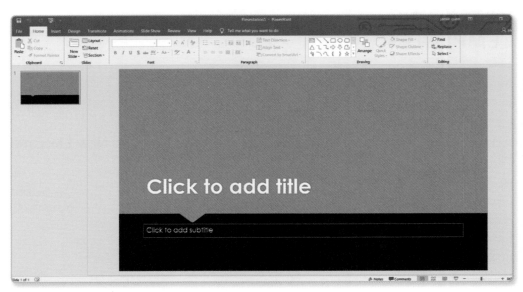

Above: Templates are pre-designed slides with generic content to be replaced by the user.

However, unlike Themes, there are a pre-determined number of slides, which are already filled with generic content. It's up to you to replace that content with your own words, pictures, images and charts, etc. As is the case with Themes, though, each template can be customized with a colour scheme and font scheme of the user's choosing.

START A NEW PRESENTATION FROM THEMES AND TEMPLATES

It's important to select your theme/template adding all of the content to your presentation. We would advise picking a theme and sticking to it, as chopping and changing can alter the appearance of your content (and not for the better). Beyond the Blank Presentation option, here is how you can select a theme or template when creating a new project.

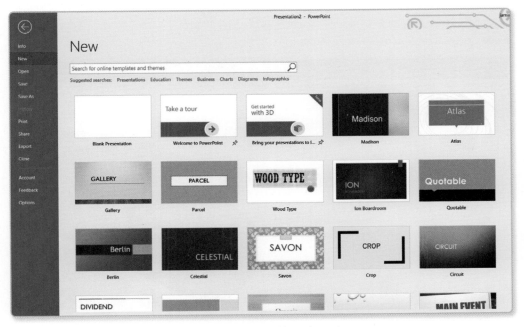

Above: There are a number of template or theme options available to choose.

PC Users: Enter the Backstage View by clicking on the File tab, then select New from the menu on the left and you'll see the available templates and themes. Choose from the options or search for a term that suits the type of presentation your want to create. Double click to select.

Mac Users: Select the File menu and click on New from Template (Command+ Shift+P) to bring up the PowerPoint Presentation Gallery. Choose from the options or search for a term that suits the type of presentation your want to create. Double click to select.

Saving Templates for future use

If you've tweaked a template or like using it you can save it to use it in future. Hit File > 'Save as type' or 'Save as template' menu and select the PowerPoint Template (.potx) option.

Below: Templates can be saved to be reused in future.

These will appear in a 'Personal' section when attempting to start a new presentation from a template in future.

Design Ideas (Office 365 subscribers only)

One of PowerPoint's better new features is the intelligent Design Ideas tool. It proactively makes design suggestions to help you improve the look and feel of your project, but you can also call on it for suggestions at any time from the Design tab. It is represented by an icon showing a lighting bolt upon a slide. Here are some options you may see. Design Ideas appear in a tab to the right

Above: Office.com templates can be downloaded for less conventional uses such as invitations or brochures.

Above: Design Ideas are an Office 365 feature that takes on screen elements and uses smart suggestions to take your slides to the next level.

- **Slide designs**: If you add a new slide, for example, Insert > New Slide > Section Header you'll get Design Ideas that will offer you variations on that type of slide.

- **Smart Art Graphics**: If you create a list of bullet points containing key dates, Design Ideas will offer to turn this into a much more attractive SmartArt graphic.

- **Illustrations**: PowerPoint scans the text within your presentation for key terms and will often suggest images from the online library to add to your presentation.

ADDING TEXT TO YOUR FIRST SLIDE

We're ready to start populating our presentation with content, starting with text, and here's how to get going with your first PowerPoint slide. We've selected the Organic theme within PowerPoint (*see* page 52), so we shall proceed using that.

WRITING YOUR FIRST SLIDE

When starting a new presentation (Control+N or Command+N on Mac), you're greeted with a single slide that appears in the Current Slide view and Slide View to the left. The slide has two text boxes, one for a title and one for a subtitle, currently filled with the words 'Click to add title' and 'Click to add subtitle'. Placing your cursor in these boxes brings up the 'I' cursor, which signifies an area where you can add text. A single click here will see the placeholder text disappear and you're ready to start typing your title.

Typing Within a Text Box

Once you've clicked within the text box you can use your computer or laptop's keyboard to start typing text. As with a word processor like Microsoft Word, words will appear on the screen as you type them. Once you reach the edges of the text box, further text will automatically move on to the next line.

Hot Tip

Try to keep the title within two lines of text to ensure that it doesn't break through the text box.

Choose a Title

The first of the two text boxes you'll see on the screen is for your title, which should encapsulate the tone and content of your presentation. For example, if you're creating a photo slide show, the title might be 'Ellie's first Christmas' (or, in our case, 'My First PowerPoint Presentation').

Add a Subtitle

A subtitle for a presentation often simply identifies the author, especially if the presentation is an academic piece of work. In that case you would click into the text box and start typing your name. However, a subtitle could clarify the content of the presentation. If your title reads: 'Getting to Grips with Microsoft PowerPoint', your subtitle might be 'From Novice to Grand Master in 2 Weeks'.

Above: Subtitles can be added to presentations to give extra information or identify the author.

Moving Between Text Boxes

Once you've added your text, you can exit a text box by moving your mouse and clicking elsewhere on the slide. If this happens to be another text box, the cursor will enter this box and you can then start editing text within it.

Adding Text to a New Content Placeholder

When adding a new slide (see opposite page), you'll see boxes within slides just waiting to be filled. These are called content placeholders and can be used to add text as well as images, pictures, videos, charts, audio and more, but the default setting is text. You can click within any content placeholder and start typing.

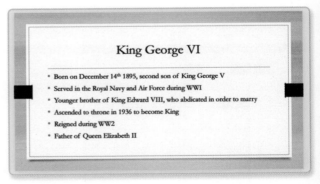

Above: The default setting for content placeholders is text, so you can just click in any placeholder box and type away.

Here PowerPoint assumes that you want to use bullet points and will arrange your text as such every time you press the Enter key. The more text you add to the box, the smaller the text will get to ensure it fits within the content box.

ADDING SLIDES TO YOUR PRESENTATION

In the previous section, we completed a text-based title page, but there's no such thing as a one-slide slide show, so in this section we'll help you add more slides and showcase the types of slides available to you.

ADDING A NEW SLIDE

The easiest way to add a default slide beneath your title page is to use the keyboard PC shortcut Control+M (Command+Shift+N on Mac). You can also click the New Slide button on the left-hand side of the Home tab. A third method is to move your cursor to the Slide View and right-click (Control+Click on Mac); this will bring up a menu from which you can select the New Slide option. This new slide will appear directly underneath the title page in the Slide View to the left of the screen and replace your title page in the Current Slide View.

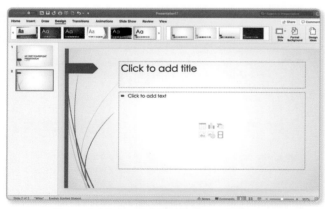

Above: A default new slide will feature a title box and multi-use content placeholder.

The Default Content Slide

Adding a new slide will automatically Add the default content slide to your presentation. This slide features a pre-set title box placed above a versatile, multiuse content placeholder, which takes up most of the page. You can click within to start typing text but you can also insert tables, charts, SmartArt, pictures and video by clicking the different options. If you feel you're ready to start adding these items, head to page 136.

SLIDE LAYOUTS

The default content slide that you see in the screenshot on the previous page is far from the only slide layout you can use. However, for our purposes of creating a basic text-based presentation it is certainly the best option.

Selecting a Layout When Adding a New Slide

In order to add a slide with a different layout, you can select the tiny down arrow beside the New Slide button within the Home tab. This will summon a drop-down menu featuring the slide layout options. From there you can hover over and click to add your selection, which will appear directly underneath the slide featured in the Current Slide view. Options include, Title and Content, Section Header, Two Content and many more.

Adding a New Layout to an Existing Slide

It's easy to customize a new or existing slide with a different layout. First of all, you'll need to identify the slide of your choosing within the Slide View tab; then right-click it and select the Layout menu to see your options. You can also achieve this by clicking the slide thumbnail to highlight it and then selecting the drop-down slide Layout menu within the Home tab.

Different Slide Layouts

We've already explained the Title Slide (*see* page 58) so some of the other pre-designed layouts you can add to a new or existing slide by hitting the Layout menu mentioned above. The Layouts will differ depending on the Themes and Templates users. Here are some of the options:

Above: Slides can be customized with new layouts by clicking on the slide and hitting Layout from the Home tab (Shown here in PowerPoint online).

- **Title and Content**: This slide will appear as the default new slide. It features a title box and one for adding content of your choosing.

Section Header: These slides usually feature the presentation name and new section title.

Two Content: A header located above two content boxes side by side.

Comparison: Similar to the above, but with further title heads; great for comparing charts or photos.

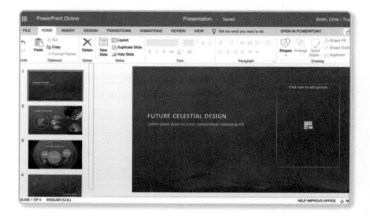

Title Only: Aside from the title, a blank canvas.

Blank: An actual blank canvas.

Above: One possible slide layout is a picture box with a caption.

Content with Caption: A title, text box and content box.

Picture with Caption: A simple way to illustrate a photo with title and corresponding text offering.

Quote with Caption: If you wish to highlight a quote, you can put it front and centre with a corresponding caption below.

Duplicating Slides

In order to save you designing the same slide over and over again, Microsoft has helpfully added this tool that will copy everything over into a new slide. All you need to do is highlight the slide in Slide View, right-click and hit Duplicate Slide – or hit Control+D (Command+D on Mac) on your keyboard. The duplicate will appear directly beneath the original.

Rearranging Your Slides

The easiest way to rearrange slides is by using the Slide Sorter view (the tiny box in the Status Bar at the bottom of the page featuring four slides), which, once selected, will replace the Normal View. Here you can grab a thumbnail by clicking on it, holding down the mouse button and dragging it into a new position within the presentation.

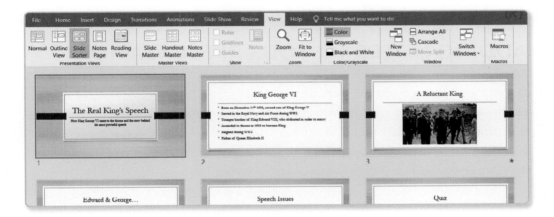

Above: The order of slides can be rearranged in the Slide Sorter view.

Deleting Slides

To get rid of a slide, just click on it within the Slide View and hit the Delete key; alternatively, right-click it and select Delete Slide. It's easy to do this by accident sometimes when you think you're editing content, so just hit the Undo shortcut Control+Z (Command+Z on Mac) to bring it safely back.

Moving Between Slides

Although you can only work on one slide at a time, you'll need to move between slides to read through your presentation and make amends. You can do this by using up/down arrow keys or by using the Slide View scroll bar. Once you reach the slide you'd like to view, simply click it.

NOTES

It's almost time to take the stage and deliver your presentation to your audience. In this section we'll cover how to add notes that will assist you with the all-important delivery.

ADDING NOTES TO YOUR PRESENTATION

As we mentioned in Chapter one, the Notes section sits neatly underneath your current slide in Normal View, with a 'Click to add notes' piece of holding text. A good set of notes can help you deliver an effective and entertaining presentation, even if the note just reads: 'Relax, remember to smile and take regular sips of water.' Notes will not appear in your presentation, and you're the only one who'll see them. The idea is to print them off (*see* page 66) as a slide-by-slide guide for when you are delivering to your audience.

How To Do It

Hover your cursor within the Notes pane, click to bring up the flashing 'I' and then begin typing. Notes are unique to each slide, rather than for the project as a whole, so try to add comments that are relevant to the content highlighted on that slide. You can treat this box as a standard word processor.

What to Put in Your Notes

Since the bullet-pointed text within your presentation features only the major points you'll need to cover, there can often be a lot of information to commit to memory. Notes can help with this. So, for example, if your bullet point reads: 'England won the World Cup in 1966', your notes could embellish with 'Bobby Moore was the captain, Geoff Hurst scored three times and they've barely come close since'. Other uses include the following:

 Jokes: Reminders to add the humorous jokes and anecdotes you had planned.

Script: You can write an entire script out to read from. Although this will limit your ability to connect with your audience, it will ensure you cover everything.

Design reminders: Notes can help you plan how to build your presentation. For example, you could add: 'Remember to insert A-ha's "Take On Me" as a soundtrack'.

Increasing the Size of the Notes Pane

The Notes pane takes up a tiny portion of the available screen space within the PowerPoint Window, which – if you're adding a lot of text – could mean a lot of scrolling. You can increase the size of the Notes pane by clicking the border just above and dragging it up. In turn this will make the current slide smaller, but you'll have more room to view your notes.

Above: The Notes pane can be increased in size to add more text.

Using Notes Page View

A more efficient alternative to altering the size of the Notes pane is to enter the Notes Page view, which features a smaller view of the slide and more space to type your notes. Select the View tab and select the Notes Page view from the left-hand side (Mac users can hit Command+3). You can return to the Normal View by hitting – you guessed it – Normal View within the Status Bar or Ribbon.

Left: Accessing the Notes Page from the View tab will give you a proper look at the notes you've made

PRINTING A PRESENTATION

Although you'll be delivering your PowerPoint presentation from a laptop screen or an external screen, print-outs of your slide show can provide a valuable reference point for your audience, who can also then take them away. A paper reference can also be useful when practising the delivery of your newly created masterpiece.

QUICK PRINT A PRESENTATION

As is the case with most features within PowerPoint, there are umpteen ways to print handouts and an almost insurmountable number of settings that can be tailored to suit to your exact needs. Luckily, there's also a way to do it with just a couple of clicks – thanks to Quick Print. As the name would suggest, this is the fastest way to commit your presentation to paper.

Above: The Print command can be found on the File Menu or Tab.

How to Quick Print

Quick Print uses the default PowerPoint print settings or, if you've changed them within the Backstage View (see below), the most recent ones. Those default settings are: one copy, all slides, one slide per page, printed in order (collated) and in colour. It won't print any of your notes or handouts.

 To Quick Print: You'll first have to add the Quick Print tool to the Quick Access Toolbar (*see* page 30) if it isn't already there. Then hit the printer icon. Naturally, your laptop or computer will need to be already configured to hook up to a printer. You'll see a brief print preview menu, where you can select Print.

Printing Using the File Tab (Backstage View on PC)

The command centre for all of your printing needs is the Backstage View within the File tab (or simply the File Menu on Mac). Hit File in the Ribbon and then the Print menu halfway down the left-hand pane. Below is the screen you'll see when preparing to print.

Printing Your Presentation on a Mac

There's no Backstage View for Mac users. Instead, you can click the printer icon in the toolbar to Quick Print or click File > Print (Command+P) to select the print settings. All of the PC options are present within a more minimalist menu, but the Quick Preview section, as it is called on the Mac, is much smaller.

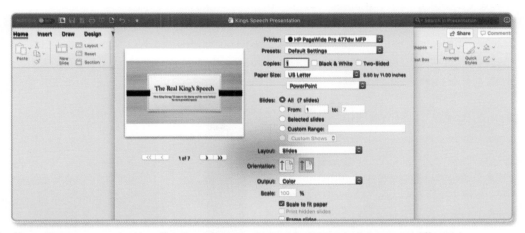

Above: The print menu on a Mac offers the same print options as on a PC, but they're presented differently.

The Print Preview View

A large part of the Print screen within the File tab is the Print Preview, which is located on the right. Not only does this show how the presentation will look on paper, but it also dynamically updates to reflect changes to the settings. For example, if you switch from colour to grayscale (see page 71) this change will be instantly reflected within the Print Preview window. You can use the scroll bar or the page turning settings beneath the preview to move between slides.

How to Print Multiple Copies

Click the up and down arrows; alternatively, click on the number 1 within the box, press delete and then type in how many copies you'd like to print.

Hot Tip

Hitting the Control+P (Command+P) keyboard short cut will take you directly to the Print settings.

Selecting a Printer

Here you can choose the printer you'd like to send the 'print job' to. Use the drop-down menu to select your printer.

Save to OneDrive and Access Online

Not everyone has a printer at home these days, but there are several ways to combat this. You can save your presentation to your OneDrive account (see page 40) or email a copy of the presentation to yourself (see page 197). That way you can access it on a computer at work, school or at the library, where there's sure to be a connected printer.

Printing All or Some Slides

Under the Settings drop-down menu section, within the Print menu, the default setting is 'Print All Slides'. If you want to print just a section of your work, select Custom Range from the drop-down menu and then enter the pages you'd like to print (for example, entering 2–5 will print pages 2, 3, 4 and 5). You can also print the Current Slide or select Print Selection. Here you'll need to enter the pages you'd like to print (for example, 1, 3 and 7).

Right: You can choose whether to print the whole presentation or only a selection of slides.

Print Layout

From the Print Settings section within the Backstage View, which currently reads 'Full Page Slides' (one slide per page), you can select how the slides appear on a printed page, but within that top line you can also choose whether to print in Notes View (see below) or Outline View (*see* page 70).

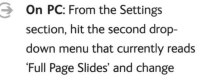

Hot Tip

The best and most common setting when printing handouts is '6 Slides Horizontal', which will put six slides on each sheet of paper with the order running from left to right.

Printing Handouts

This setting is also controlled from the drop-down Layout menu headed 'Slides'. Here you'll see a Handouts menu that allows you to select how many slides appear on the page. You can also tick a box that will add black frames to each slide, one which will scale up the slides to fill more of the page and another that will print high-quality versions of the slides.

Printing Your Notes Page

The whole point of having a Notes section is to print them out so you can use them while making the presentation. In order to do this, you need to select the File tab and click the Print option.

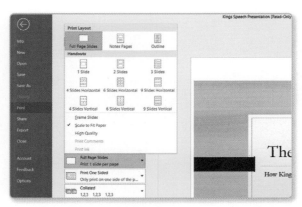

Above: For handouts, printing six slides ordered horizontally on a page is a good option.

➡ **On PC**: From the Settings section, hit the second drop-down menu that currently reads 'Full Page Slides' and change that to Notes Pages. Hit the Print button and a beautiful set of notes featuring a thumbnail of each slide shall be yours.

➡ **On a Mac:** Hit File > Print and browse to the Layout section that reads slides. Hit the drop down menu and select Notes.

Above: Notes pages can be printed out to help the speaker when giving the presentation (Shown here in PowerPoint online).

Printing in Outline View

Working in Outline view is something we'll cover in Chapter three, but we should mention here that printing in Outline View gives you a better view of the content within your slides, rather than the slides themselves. This can be a useful way to print in order to practise your presentation.

➡ **On a PC:** Simply Print from the BackStage View and browse to Settings. Hit the dropdown menu and click Outline on the top row of options.

➡ **On a Mac:** Hit File > Print. Browse to Layout, hit the drop down menu and select Outline.

Collating Your Print Job

The Collated setting is useful if you're printing multiple copies of your presentation. The default

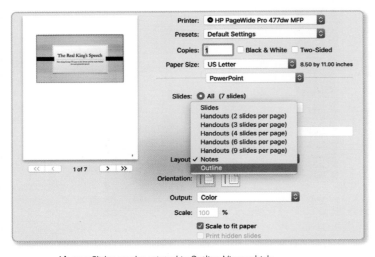

Above: Slides can be printed in Outline View, which focuses on the slide content (shown here on a Mac).

'Collated' setting is to print the pages in order (for example, 1,2,3, 1,2,3, and so on). Changing this setting to Uncollated will mean that all of the page ones will be printed followed by all of the page twos, etc.

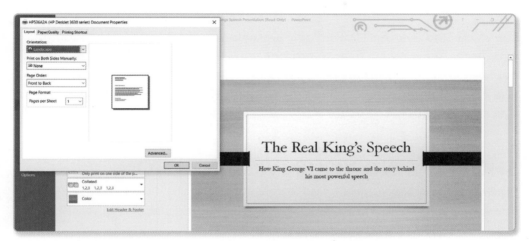

Above: Choose to print in either portrait or landscape orientation depending on your use.

Print Orientation

Select whether you'd like your slides to be printed in Portrait Orientation (vertically) or in Landscape Orientation (horizontally) on the paper. If you're printing single slides, the default landscape view maximizes paper space, but if you're printing handouts or notes, we'd suggest portrait as the best option.

A Slice of Colour

Have you seen how much colour printer cartridges cost these days? In most cases, selecting the 'Grayscale' (uses grey shades rather than whites) or 'Pure Black and White' options will suffice for your handouts.

Hot Tip

If you're opting to submit a print-out of your PowerPoint presentation as an academic piece of work then go for the full colour option – first impressions count!

PREPARING YOUR PRESENTATION FOR DELIVERY

You've created your first PowerPoint presentation, printed the handouts, got your notes and now it's time to present it. In this section we'll look at the best way to screen your presentation depending on your audience; we will also offer some guidance on rehearsing it and give some vital tips to ensure that the end product of your hard work is truly appreciated and enjoyed by all.

SHOWCASING YOUR PRESENTATION

Depending on your audience, you'll need to make a decision on how best to showcase your slide show. If you're delivering to one or two people then there's no doubt that your laptop or desktop monitor is a sufficient presentation tool.

However, if you have an audience of work colleagues then you may want to hook up to an external monitor (like a flatscreen TV), and if you're speaking to a packed lecture theatre or conference hall then you'll definitely need the assistance of a projector linked to your computer.

Using a Computer or Laptop Screen

This is the easy part. You simply have to select the Slide Show view from the Status Bar in order to fill your screen with the PowerPoint presentation. This will minimize all toolbars, options, other views and menus, and simply display the slides.

Left: In Slideshow View the presentation will fill the screen.

HDMI

Most recent laptops and all high definition televisions (HDTVs) or projectors have HDMI (High Definition Multimedia Interface) connection, which is the easiest – and most modern – way to link your laptop or computer to a television set. An HDMI cable can transmit pictures and sound from one to the other at higher quality than a VGA (Video Graphics Array) cable (see below). HDMI cables are inexpensive and durable. To ensure your computer or laptop has a HDMI output

Above: The HDMI port on a laptop.

check the body for the port marked HDMI (it is shaped like the photo above). If your computer doesn't have a HDMI adapter like many new Mac laptops, you can buy an adapter.

Other Ports?

No HDMI outlet? Your computer will still be able to link up with a TV, projector or external monitor thanks to some ports.

- **VGA:** Older laptops, projectors and screens have VGA ports. These 15-pin cables will transmit pictures but not sound, so you may need to add speakers to your computer to project sound.

- **USB-C/Thunderbolt 3**: Newer laptops feature the smaller, more versatile USB-C ports that enable direct connection to a compatible monitor (these are often called Thunderbolt ports). You can also use an adapter to connect to HDMI.

- **DVI**: Rather than VGA ports, Macs use Digital Visual Interface (DVI) outputs, meaning you may need an adapter as well as a cable to link to the ports on your TV or projector.

⊖ **DisplayPort/Mini DisplayPort**: Some laptops rely on DisplayPort technology over HDMI technology. Many external monitors support this standard. Otherwise you'll need an adapter to connect with an external screen.

⊖ **Wireless**: There are a number of wireless technologies that enables you to hook up to the TV, monitor or projector. Apple's AirPlay (with an Apple TV box) is one that Mac users may opt for. Others monitors may have wireless screen mirroring capabilities.

Configuring Your Computer to Work on a HDTV

Connect your laptop or computer to your TV via HDMI or VGA and then use the Input button on your TV remote control to select the relevant channel. When using HDMI, the correct input will be HDMI (followed by the number of the input, e.g. HDMI2), whereas the VGA channel will likely be called 'PC' or 'Computer'.

From there, your PC should automatically recognize the presence of the TV but to tailor the settings hit Start > Control Panel > Hardware and Sound > Displays > Connect to an external display in order to bring up the dialogue box below. Depending on the PC you're using, these settings may be slightly different. Apple Mac users can adjust the display settings by selecting System Preferences > Displays.

> # Hot Tip
> Head to https://support.apple.com/ en-us/HT202351 for full details on how to connect your Mac to an external display.

Configuring Your Computer to Work with a Projector

Once you've connected the source and destination machine with an HDMI or VGA cable, you'll need to use the projector's remote to select the correct video input (like the TV, it'll be called HDMI or PC). From here you should see an indication on the projected screen that the two devices are connected.

Mirroring or extending displays (PC Only)

The default setting will be to mirror your display on the television. However, there's more to configure here. You can choose to extend the display so the presentation only appears on the external screen.

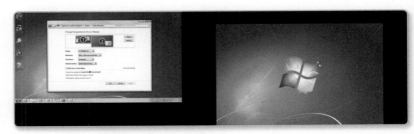

Above: Different display options can be chosen.

Hot Tip

When connected to a projector, hit the Windows key + P to enter Presentation Mode (PC only).

Click the Start button and enter the Settings menu and click the System icon. Here you'll see Advanced Display Settings. Here you should see the two monitors represented on screen. If not, select 'Detect' and wait for it to be picked up. Here you'll see additional options:

- **Computer only**: Shows nothing on the projector screen and everything on your computer display.

- **Duplicate**: As the name suggests, this will mirror the same content on both screens.

- **Show only on 1**: Choose this before you're ready to start presenting

- **Show only on 2**: Show your presentation only on the secondary display. The laptop screen will go black. This is great if you're presenting in a darkened room.

Above: These options dictate what content will be shown on the computer and projector screens.

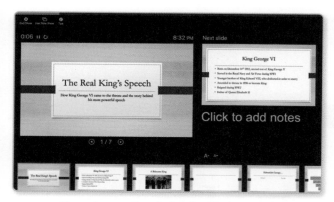

Above: Presenter View displays the slide show on a monitor and allows it to be commanded from the computer.

Selecting Presenter View

When PowerPoint detects that an external monitor has been connected, be it a HDTV or a projector, you'll be able to push the slide show itself on to the new display while commanding the presentation from your laptop screen. This is called Presenter View (select the Slide Show tab and tick 'Use Presenter View'); for a detailed explanation on how to use this *see* page 83.

All the tools needed to make the final preparations before delivering your slide show reside in the Slide Show tab within the Ribbon. From here you can play your slide show from various points within the presentation, create a custom slide show, go hands-free and more.

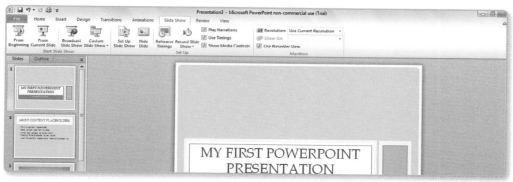

Above: The Slide Show tab allows for final preparations to be made to the presentation.

Start Slide Show from Beginning

This tool, within the Slide Show tab, can be used when performing or practising your presentation. Hitting From Beginning/Play From Start (on Mac) will play the presentation in full.

You can move between the slides manually (*see* page 81) or automatically by adding timings (see Rehearse Timings on page 79).

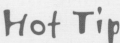

Start Slide Show from Current Slide

Selecting this tool is a great option if you've built a long presentation and don't want to show it all or just want to practice a certain section without viewing the whole thing. Simply click once on the slide of your choice and then select 'From Current Slide' within the Slide Show tab in the Ribbon.

Hot Tip

Press F5 on a PC (Command+Shift+ Return on a Mac) to begin your presentation from the first slide, from anywhere within PowerPoint.

Broadcast Slide Show

This isn't something we'll analyse in-depth at present, but PowerPoint 2010 allows you to give a presentation for online viewers to tune into (*see* page 208).

Custom Slide Show

Rather than spending all that time rearranging and duplicating (*see* page 62 for more information on both), you can create a custom slide show by placing slides in a specific order for presentation and repeating them if necessary. Click Custom Slide Show > Custom Shows > New (+ sign on Mac) and transfer the slides across one by one, by highlighting them and clicking Add. When you have finished, click OK and then Show to view the presentation in that order.

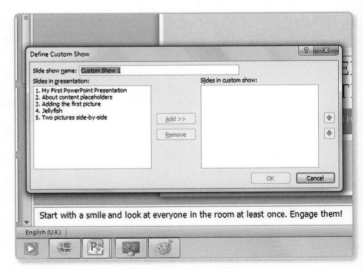

Above: Slides can be chosen, reordered and repeated to create custom shows.

SETTING UP YOUR SLIDE SHOW

The options in the centre of the Slide Show tab feature some more advanced presentation settings. In Chapter five, we'll discuss how to turn your presentation into a recorded video with audio narrations and highlighting through an on-screen laser pointer. Firstly, though, let's take a look at some of the more basic functionality available here.

The 'Set Up Show' Window

This pop-up dialogue box, which is accessed by hitting 'Set Up Slide Show' in the Slide Show tab, features some basic and some of the more advanced functionality to be covered later. The following represent what is most relevant to us at present.

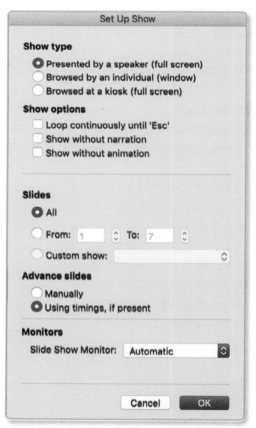

Above: The Set Up Show menu allows control over how slides are changed and whether to run the presentation on a loop.

- **Show type:** Choose between Presented by a speaker (full screen), Browsed by an individual (window) and Browsed at a kiosk (window), depending on where your show will be displayed.

- **Show options:** For a presentation that will continue to run, for example at an information station, you can select the Loop continuously until 'Esc', meaning that it will continue to run until someone presses Escape on the keyboard to end the show.

- **Advance slides:** Select whether to move through slides by hand or via the pre-selected timings (if present), which will enable you to go hands-free and 'work the room'. We'll come to that shortly.

From this menu, you'll also be able to control whether narrations and animations play, the colour of your pen (when drawing) and the colour of the laser pointer (when pointing); additionally, you can select the Custom Show setting and adjust the external monitors settings (*see* page 75).

Hide Slide

Back within the Slide Show tab, this option simply hides one or more selected slides so that they won't be shown within the live presentation. They will not be deleted; they just won't appear in the show. It's great if you plan to use a presentation multiple times but feel that certain slides are not relevant to your audience. In order to undo this, simply right-click the hidden slide's thumbnail and deselect the Hide Slide box.

Rehearse Timings

Using this tool is a great way to give your presentation automatically without having to manually advance the slides. Hitting Rehearse Timings in the Slide Show tab will automatically launch the slide show and start a stopwatch in the top-left corner of the presentation.

Above: A stopwatch (top left of screen) will run on screen so that the presentation can be rehearsed and timings worked out.

The idea is for you to deliver the presentation as you would on your big stage. When you're ready to move to the next slide or bullet point, hit Enter (or the down arrow on your keyboard) and PowerPoint will remember how long you spent on this slide. Continue this process throughout the presentation and when you're finished, press Escape on PC or the End Show button on Mac.

Now you'll have the full presentation recorded. You can review how long you spent on each clip by clicking the Slide Sorter view within the Status Bar. If you're unhappy, you can hit Rehearse Timings again to have another go.

With the recording complete, selecting the Use Timings option from the Slide Show Ribbon tab will free you up to focus on the content rather than the technology when the time comes to address your audience.

DELIVERING YOUR PRESENTATION

You should now be ready for the most important part of this process: presenting to your audience. Here are the tools you'll need to pull it off successfully.

STARTING YOUR PRESENTATION

Regardless of the screen you're using to present your slide show (*see* pages 76–77), you'll need to press Start Slide Show from Beginning (or alternatively hit the F5 key Command+Shift+Return on Mac) from the Slide Show tab to kick things off. Once you've taken the plunge, you're ready to start moving through the slides and engaging your audience.

Important Keyboard and Mouse Tools

Here are the key navigational tools, using both the mouse and the trackpad, when presenting your slide show to the audience.

- **To move to next point/animation/slide**: Press enter; hit the space bar; use the down arrow; hit the 'N' key; hit page down; click your left mouse button; use the on-screen right arrow beneath the presentation (Mac and PC).

- **To move to previous point/animation/slide**: Press Backspace; use the up arrow; hit the 'P' key; press page up; click the right mouse button and select 'Previous'; use the on-screen left arrow beneath the presentation (Mac and PC).

- **To return to start**: Press 1+Enter (Return on a Mac); right-click; select Go to Slide and enter 1 when prompted; hold down both mouse buttons (Mac and PC).

➔ **To jump to slide**: Press the slide number + Enter (for example, 9 + Enter).

➔ **To pause/resume manual slide show**: Press the S key (Mac and PC); right-click and hit pause/restart (PC).

➔ **To send screen to white or black**: If you'd like to pause and remove content from the screen for a while, you can make the screen black or white. Press 'B' for Black and 'W' for white, and hit the same key to bring the content back (Mac and PC).

➔ **To end the slide show**: Press the Escape key (Mac and PC).

Using the Laser Pointer

In order to activate the laser pointer, you'll need both your keyboard and your trackpad/ mouse. Once you start the presentation you can click the pen icon in the bottom left corner. Here you'll see the laser pointer option. Select it and your cursor will become a red dot. Alternatively, press Control, hold down the left mouse button and drag. Mac users can also press the Command+L keyboard shortcut.

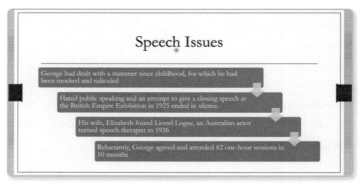

Above: The laser pointer helps you focus your audience's attention on the element of display you're discussing.

Hot Tip

To change the colour of the laser pointer, click on **Set Up Slide Show** in the Slide Show Ribbon tab and select 'Laser pointer colour'. You can choose between red (the default), green or blue.

How to Draw on Your Slides

In order to activate the pen tool, simply press Control+P (Command+P on Mac) while you're within your presentation, as this will change the arrow cursor into a pen. You can also right-click, select Pointer Options and then Pen (or, if you're on a PC, you can also select Highlighter so as not to draw over slides).

Hot Tip

You might consider it unthinkable to use a pen tool, which would spoil your lovely slides, but it could come in handy to circle a particular stat or emphasize a particular point.

ABOUT CONTENT PLACEHOLDERS

- This is a content placeholder
- Here we can add text to slides
- Which can appear as bullet points
- Pressing Enter produces a new bullet
- Most PowerPoint presentations feature bulleted lists

Above: Certain information on slides can be emphasized with the pen tool.

Once you see the pen icon replace the arrow cursor, simply hold down the left mouse button and scribble away by moving the mouse or trackpad. Pressing the E key will delete your doodles, while a single press of the Escape key returns the cursor to the arrow pointer (be careful, as two presses will exit presentation mode completely).

USING PRESENTER VIEW

If you're presenting using an external monitor, it allows you to display your presentation slides full screen by using the television or projector you're hooked up to, while still accessing a full control panel on your host desktop or laptop computer.

When accessing Presenter View, ensure your computer is connected to the external monitor (*see* pages 73–75). The presentation won't immediately load on to the external monitor but you'll see it appear on your television or projector when you hit Presenter View from the Slide Show menu.

The Presenter View Window

With the first slide now present on your external monitor, your PC screen will then be furnished with the Presenter View which means you will see the following:

1. Current slide (left) so you can see what's on screen.
2. Slide show thumbnails (top right) so you know what's coming next.
3. The Notes pane (bottom right) so you can keep reminders of your talking points.

All the mouse and keyboard commands mentioned on pages 81–82 still work in Presenter View; you can also draw and use the laser pointer (PC only) on the 'Current Slide' pane, and your movements will be translated to the big screen as you make them. You will also be able to see the following.

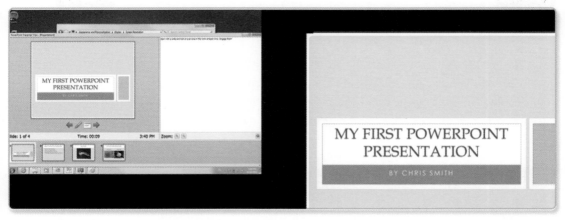

Above: The computer screen will display various aspects of the presentation whilst the external monitor displays only the slides.

Slide count: for example, 'Slide: 4 of 7'.

Time of presentation: How long your presentation has been running.

Play/Pause: If you want to halt your presentation for questions, you can hit the pause button in Presenter View and then hit play to recommence.

Time: The actual time of day. Great if you're working in a classroom setting and need to finish by a certain time. Left and right arrows: Use these to move between slides.

Pen icon: Hit this to select all of the arrow options (arrow pen, highlighter, ink colour).

Slide show: Effectively, this represents a right click and houses commands such as next slide, previous slide, pause, end show, etc.

Zoom: Use small and large A icons to increase and decrease the size of texts in the notes.

Keeping Your Display Awake

To ensure your computer or your external monitor does not go to sleep leaving you with a blank screen when delivering a presentation, hit 'Start' and type 'sleep' in the search box. Select Power and Sleep settings and select how long the computer waits before entering sleep mode. On a Mac choose System Preferences > Power Adapter and alter the 'Turn the display off after' settings.

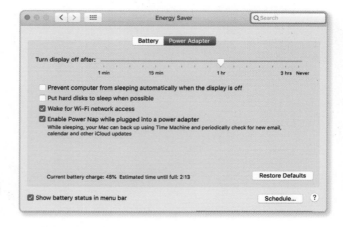

Above: It's important to make sure your display doesn't automatically go to sleep during a presentation.

IMPROVING A PRESENTATION

EDITING TEXT

After completing your presentation, it's likely that you'll want to make changes, additions and corrections to your text. In some cases, you'll want to delete it completely and start certain sections over again – here's how.

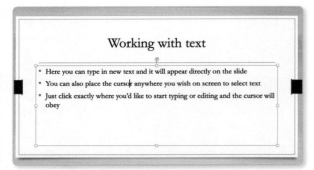

Above: Place your cursor where you want to start editing, click, and start typing.

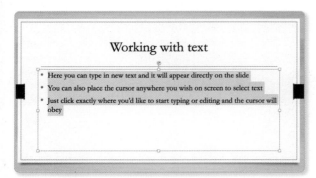

Above: Text can be selected by holding down the left mouse button and dragging the cursor over it.

ADDING TEXT

Just like when you were first adding text to a content placeholder, you can click within the box to select and edit text. The 'I' cursor will appear within the text closest to where you clicked, so if you want to edit from the end of the section, point your cursor immediately after the last word and click.

Selecting text

There are plenty of ways to highlight sections of text, or all text within a content box. Sometimes you might want to simply change the size or the colour of a certain piece of text, other times you might want to delete it all and start again.

- **To select a single word**: Double-click the mouse or trackpad on that word.

- **To select a paragraph**: Triple-click a word within the text box.

To select all text: Use the keyboard shortcut Control+A (Command+A on a Mac).

Deleting Text

Select the relevant section of text and then press Backspace (Delete on Mac) to remove it. If you want to delete a single word or to correct a spelling, you can place your 'I' cursor directly behind that word or letter and press Backspace to delete one letter at a time.

Amending Text

In order to amend text, just click your cursor where you'd like to add the text and start writing; this will add to the content placeholder rather than overwrite what is already there.

Adding a New Bullet Point

As we explained in Chapter two (*see* page 59), whenever you press Enter within a text box, a new bullet point will be added directly underneath. If you'd like to insert a new bullet point within a content placeholder, place your 'I' cursor at the end of the sentence above where you'd like the next point to appear and hit Enter; this will push those underneath down.

Hot Tip

In order to select a paragraph of text, hit your left mouse button three times in quick succession.

Working with text

in new text and it will appear directly on the slide

the cursor anywhere you wish on screen to selec

here you'd like to start typing or edit|

Above: Backspace removes text to the left of the cursor, while Delete removes text to the right.

Hot Tip

Backspace will remove text from right to left (anticlockwise), while the Delete (Fn+Delete on Mac) key will wipe out text from left to right (clockwise).

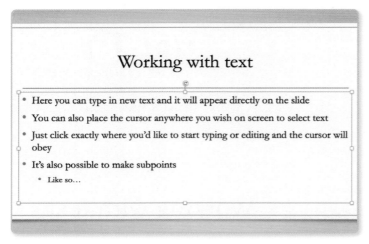

Above: It is easy to create sub-points within a bulleted list.

Adding Sub-points and Multiple Paragraph Levels

You can also use this tool to create sub-points (or second-level points) within the list. Hit Enter at the end of a bullet point and then press Tab on the keyboard; this will indent the next point. You can do this multiple times.

CUT, COPY AND PASTE

The Cut, Copy and Paste tools are three of the most useful PowerPoint commands. They allow you to take text (or any other object) from one location, store it on a virtual clipboard and then paste it elsewhere within your presentation.

Copying Text to the Clipboard

Use the instructions on pages 88–89 to highlight the area of text you wish to copy. Once you're happy with your selection, you can use the keyboard shortcut Control+C (Command+C on a Mac) to copy it to the virtual clipboard.

Multiple Clipboard items (PC Only)

If you've copied multiple items, you can access them all on the PowerPoint Clipboard (see across the page), which stores all of your recent copies. You can access the Clipboard view by selecting it from the Home tab. Clicking on an item within the Clipboard will paste it on to the slide in Current Slide View.

Cutting Text

The Cut tool has the same effect as Copy, in that it still copies the selected text to the Clipboard. However, in this case it also removes the text from the source. While Copy is best when used for duplicating text elsewhere, Cut is more efficient if you want to move a section of text from one slide to another. In order to access the Cut tool, select the section of text and hit the keyboard short cut Control+X (Command+X on Mac).

Pasting Text

Once you've copied or cut the relevant text to the Clipboard (see above), you can paste it elsewhere into the PowerPoint presentation. Simply position the cursor within the content placeholder and hit Control+V (Command+V on a Mac) and the text will appear, as if by magic, directly after where you placed the cursor.

Deleting it All

If you want the whole content placeholder gone from your slide, use your mouse to click on the border and then hit Backspace or Delete and it'll be

Above: The clipboard gives you easy access to recently copied items.

Hot Tip

When copying, cutting and pasting text, right-click the highlighted sections and hit the relevant command. Icon buttons for all three also appear in the Home Ribbon tab on PCs and Macs.

Hot Tip

These Cut, Copy and Paste commands are universal across Microsoft Office, so they're ideal for copying text pre-prepared in a Word document and pasting it into a PowerPoint slide.

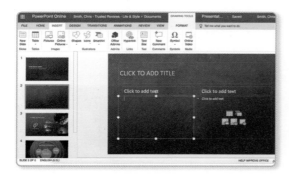

Left: Clicking on the border of a content placeholder selects it so that you can delete it (Shown here in PowerPoint online).

gone. However, if you do this by accident, read the section below, as this can rescue you. If you'd like to cut, copy and paste the text elsewhere, use the tools mentioned above.

UNDOING MISTAKES

There's nothing worse than the thought that, through some momentary insanity, you've deleted all of your beautifully crafted text. When messing around with Cut, Copy and Paste tools, these moments of panic can become common.

The Undo Tool

Thankfully, all is not lost as there is an easy fix to bring your work back. This tool works across the software, so keep it in mind if you delete a slide by accident, add a theme you don't like, change a font or decide a particular picture doesn't work.

Hit the back arrow in the Quick Access Toolbar to jump back one step or use the Undo keyboard shortcut Control+Z (Command+Z on a Mac).

Hot Tip

The small down arrow next to the Undo command will launch a menu that allows you to jump several steps back at a time – perfect if you're unhappy with a recent change of direction.

The Redo Tool

The Redo tool comes in handy if you've used Undo (see opposite) to take a step back but want to redo the undo. The keyboard shortcut is Control+Y (Command+Y for Mac) but you can also use the toolbar arrow next to Undo. On PC, Drop-down arrows in the toolbar allow you to jump forward several steps.

Don't Save It

If you're unhappy with your afternoon's work and want to start again from your last save, simply close the presentation (*see* page 42) and select 'Don't Save'. Then you can reopen the document to return to the last save (*see* page 43).

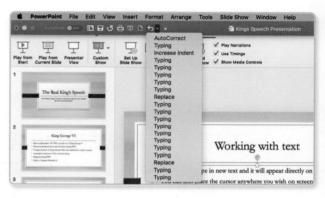

Above: The Undo command allows you to undo several actions in one go.

FINDING TEXT WITHIN YOUR PRESENTATION

If you know the piece of text you'd like to amend but don't want to spend ages poring through each slide to locate it, you can use PowerPoint's built-in finder tool. You can type in the word of your choice and PowerPoint will highlight each of the destinations where that word or phrase appears. Select one to go straight to it.

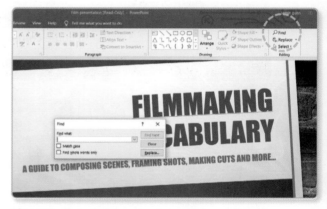

Above: The finder tool makes locating particular words much quicker than scanning by eye.

On PC: The search tool lives within the Editing pane of the Home tab in the PowerPoint Ribbon. Select the magnifying glass (or use Control+F) to bring up the Find window.

On a Mac: Apple users have the advantage of an omnipresent Search in Presentation bar at the top right corner of the PowerPoint Window. You can also use Command+F.

Find and Replace

This tool very is useful if you know that there's something you'd like to correct multiple times throughout the presentation.

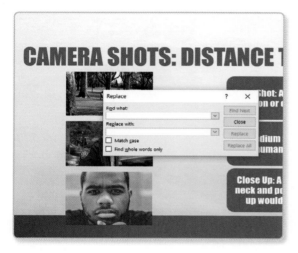

Above: The find and replace tool on a Mac is very useful for correcting something several times.

→ **On a PC**: Press Control+F to bring up the Find window and hit the Replace button. Type a word (e.g. Powerpoint) into the 'Find what' box and type the correct replacement (e.g. PowerPoint) within the 'Replace with' box, and then click the 'Replace All' button.

→ **On a Mac**: Use the drop-down arrow on the Search in Presentation bar in the PowerPoint Window and follow the instructions above.

SPELLCHECKING YOUR WORK

If your presentation is littered with spelling errors, this will immediately undermine your authority. Thankfully, for those of us whose brain wasn't fitted with the complete Oxford Dictionary software, there are numerous tools to ensure everything is accurate.

Spellchecking as You Type

If PowerPoint believes you've spelled something incorrectly it will underline it in red. Right-click the word; if PowerPoint has suggestions for the correct spelling you will see them listed in the pop-up menu. Hover over the correct spelling and click it. This action will replace the incorrect word with the correct one.

Spellchecker in the Status Bar (PC Only)

Within the Status Bar, at the very bottom of the PowerPoint Window, there is a small box that indicates whether spelling errors are present within your work. If there are no errors a tick will appear over the open book, whereas if there are errors that need your attention you'll see a red cross.

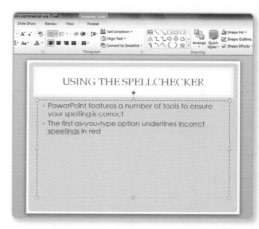

Summoning the Spelling Tool

Beyond the red cross and red underline, you can check your spelling by selecting Review from the Ribbon and then hitting the nice big spelling button (which says 'ABC' and has a big tick beneath it).

Above: PowerPoint can check your spelling by underlining errors in red.

Using the Spelling Tool

Let's imagine that in our presentation we've incorrectly spelled Microsoft as 'Mircosoft' and from the Window you can see that the software is suggesting we change it to Microsoft or perhaps the word Mycroft. Here's an explanation of the tools we can use here.

Ignore: Hit this button if you're happy with how the word is spelled. This will stop PowerPoint assuming that the word is spelled incorrectly.

Ignore All: If the word appears multiple times during the document, hitting this button will tell PowerPoint that you're happy with how it's spelled throughout the presentation.

Change: Hitting this button will change the word to the one listed in the 'Change to' box.

Change all: Will change the incorrectly spelled word to the highlighted suggestion throughout the document.

Add: Use this button to add a word PowerPoint thinks is incorrectly spelled to your dictionary, so that the software recognizes it next time.

Completing the Spellcheck

Once you've addressed all of the errors that PowerPoint thinks you've made, the Spelling window will be replaced with a notification that the 'Spelling check is complete' – hit OK and continue with your work.

Above: Words can be added to the PowerPoint dictionary to be recognized in future.

AutoCorrecting Your Spelling

Occasionally, when you're typing within PowerPoint, you'll notice that the software automatically changes your text after you've finished writing a word. To access the full range of AutoCorrect options hit File > Options > Proofing > AutoCorrect Options (Tools > AutoCorrect Options on Mac).

> # Hot Tip
> You can also right-click on a word and select Add To Dictionary, which means PowerPoint (along with Word, Excel, OneNote and all Office programs) will add it to your custom dictionary and recognize it in future.

Show AutoCorrect Options buttons: If PowerPoint AutoCorrects your text it will, by default, present a little lightning bolt beneath the word that gives you the option of overriding the changes or stop correcting that particular word.

Correct TWo INitial CApitals: This will make those unwanted second capital letters in a word go away.

Capitalize first letter of sentences/table cells: Some basic grammar help.

➔ **Capitalize names of days:**
No one wants to make grammar errors on a thursday.

➔ **Correct accidental use of cAPS LOCK key:** This often happens when a user attempts to hit the shift key in order to capitalize the first letter of a word.

➔ **Replace text as you type:** Ensuring this box is ticked enables PowerPoint's vast library of commonly misspelled words to end a helping hand.

➔ **Exceptions:** Adjacent to the first two options in this menu, you'll see a box that says Exceptions. Here you can add items where you don't want the first letter to be capitalized (e.g. anon.) and where using two capitals at the start of the word (e.g. IDs) is actually correct.

➔ **Replace/With:** As you can see, this list shows a list of commonly used symbols such as ©, which is actually typed as (C), and ™, which is typed as (TM). You can use the tools in there to add your own items or delete from this list.

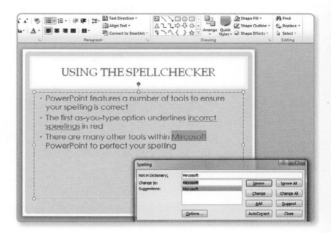

Above: PowerPoint offers suggestions for correcting the misspelt word.

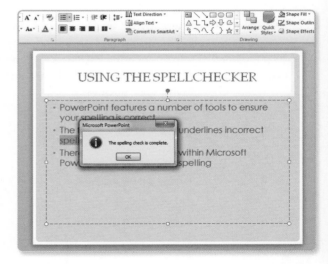

Above: The spellchecker will let you know when it is complete.

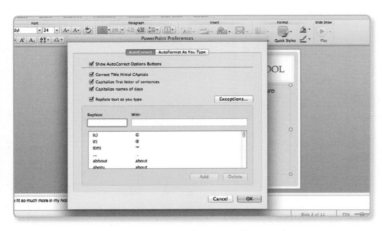

Above: You can choose your preferences for how spelling mistakes are automatically corrected.

Hot Tip

PowerPoint's suggestions won't always be right, especially if you're using colloquial terms and proper nouns such as place names. If you're unhappy with a correction just press Control+Z (Command+Z) to undo it and move on with your business.

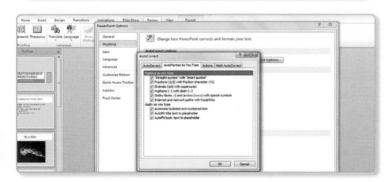

Above: You will be presented with options such as replacing hyphens with dashes.

Using AutoFormat

While we're within the AutoCorrect options, it's a good time to take a look at the AutoFormat As You Type tab. This controls the AutoCorrect options outside of spelling and capitalization, such as when to hyphenate words or add internet hyperlinks. You can see the options in the screenshot to the left.

Apply as You Type Settings

From the window mentioned above you can also control whether PowerPoint automatically adds bullet points and numbered lists, whether to AutoFit title text to placeholder (PC only) and whether to AutoFit body text to placeholder.

Making Use of the Thesaurus

The Thesaurus tool is perfect for checking the meanings of words and finding alternatives (synonyms) to terms we use too often. On PC, you can access the Thesaurus by right-clicking on the word of your choice and selecting Synonyms to reveal alternatives. Then select the word you prefer to replace it.

However, there's also a handy Thesaurus tool next to spelling in the Review tab within the Ribbon. Highlight the word of your choice and click Thesaurus from the left hand side. This will bring up a number of suggestions, if PowerPoint had them in its arsenal.

Reference Tools

Right-click a word and select Smart Look Up to launch the Reference Tools toolbar. Here you will have the chance to look up a dictionary definition of the word, an audio clip with the correct pronunciation and to access online research tools like Bing and Wikipedia.

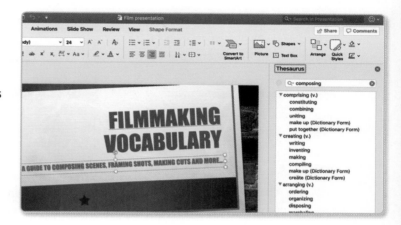

Above: If you need an alternative to a word used too often, the Thesaurus can offer suggestions.

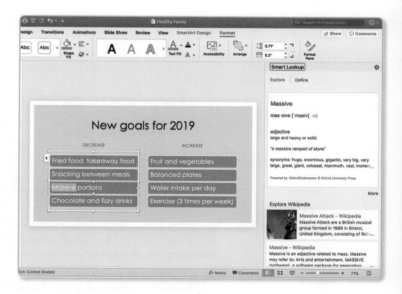

Above: The Reference task pane includes handy tools such as a dictionary and thesaurus.

Translate your presentation

If you have a multi-lingual audience, PowerPoint has the tools required to alter the language of your text. All you need to do is highlight the text in question and hit the Translate tab in the Review ribbon.

This will give you options to select a new language. After selecting from the drop-down menu, simply press insert to replace your English text with the new language.

Hot Tip

If your PowerPoint default language is English (U.K.) instead of English (U.S.) the software will think you've made a host of spelling errors. Altering the proofing language within the Language window in the Review tab will let PowerPoint know that you mean to 'customize' rather than 'customize' your language.

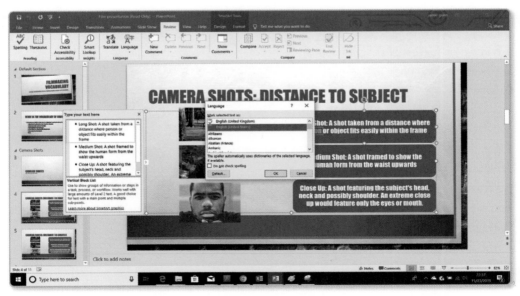

Above: Make sure you are set up in the right language or PowerPoint will mistakenly think you have made spelling errors.

FORMATTING TEXT

Now that your text is spotless in terms of language, spelling and grammar, we can think about making it a little bolder, a little braver and a little prettier. Within the next few pages, you'll find plenty of information on improving the look and feel of your text.

TEXT EMPHASIS TOOLS

When editing text, you'll notice that the Home tab features most of the same formatting tools you'll see in a word processor like Microsoft Word. Some of the basic ones are listed below. In the Home tab, PowerPoint offers a rich variety of text formatting tools.

➲ **Bold:** Makes your text appear darker and slightly thicker. It's ideal to give single words emphasis or to identify titles. Select text and click the B icon in the Ribbon or hit Control+B (Command+B on Mac).

➲ *Italic:* Select text and hit the slanted I icon or the short cut Control+I (Command+I on Mac) to add emphasis to words or sentences.

➲ <u>Underlined:</u> Use the U icon or hit the short cut Control+U (Command+U on Mac).

Above: You can emphasize text by making it bold, italic or underlined.

INCREASING AND DECREASING FONT SIZE

Sometimes it's necessary within PowerPoint to change the size of your text in order for it to fill out or make more room within your content placeholder. As always, with PowerPoint there are numerous ways to do this, but first of all you'll need to highlight the relevant text (*see* page 88).

The best way to steadily increase the size of your text is to use the dedicated buttons within the Ribbon. The font size icons (see in the screenshot above) will either increase or decrease the size of the text. You can also use the keyboard short cuts Control+Shift+> to increase or Control+Shift+< to decrease text sizes. Alternatively, you can change the font size by using the drop-down menu that displays the current size.

Hot Tip

Hitting the drop-down menu gives you a number of underline options to choose from (dotted, double underline, etc.).

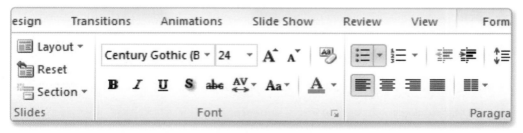

Above: The increase and decrease icons allow you to steadily change the size of your text.

TEXT ALIGNMENT

Text alignment concerns how your words will appear within the PowerPoint content placeholders in which they sit. There are four key options within the Paragraph section of the Home tab.

Hot Tip

Don't make your text too small just to fit it on a slide. Instead, consider adding a new slide to make room.

- **Align Text Left**: The first word will hug the left edge of the box.

- **Centre Text**: Places text equidistantly from the left and right edges of the content placeholder, with the middle letter anchoring the centre.

- **Align Text Right**: The last word will hug the right edge of the box.

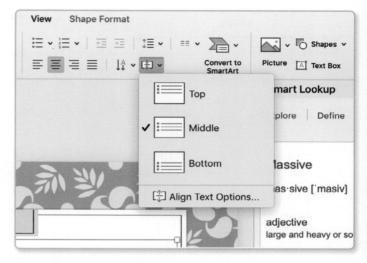

Above: There are a number of options for where words can sit in the content placeholders.

- **Justify Text**: This option spaces the text out to ensure that the words are spread out evenly across the line.

Vertical Text Alignment

You can also select the Align Text box within the Home tab to choose whether your words are anchored to the top, bottom or centre of the content placeholder.

Text Direction

In the West we generally read and write from left to right, but in PowerPoint, anything goes. You may want a title to run from the top to the bottom of the page, or from the bottom to the top, for the purpose of building a heading (see below). Before you go flipping your words on their heads, though, you'll need to ensure that your content placeholder has been designed (*see* page 128) in a way that would accommodate vertically aligned text; however, if that's up to scratch, you can select from four options within the drop-down box (see screenshot above).

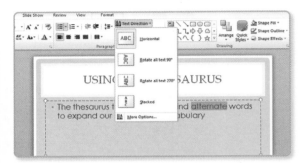

Above: You are not limited to having your text run from left to right.

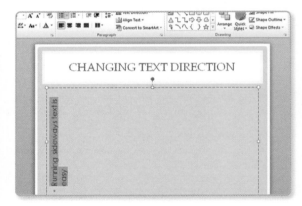

Above: Text can be rotated to enable you to have sideways headings..

Hot Tip

Once you've made these changes and your text is running in the right direction, you may want to use the Align Text tab to ensure the words hug the correct portion of the content placeholder.

Horizontal: The default text layout.

Rotate all text 90°: Will change your text to run vertically from topto bottom.

Rotate all text 270°: Will change your text to run vertically from the bottom of the content placeholder to the top.

Stacked: This hardly ever looks good (try it if you don't believe us). It will place all letters on top of each other.

BULLET POINTS AND NUMBERED LISTS

You may have noticed when writing within content placeholders that each time you press Enter, a new bullet point is created, as PowerPoint assumes that most text slides will feature a number of bulleted talking points.

In order to turn a text passage into bullet points or a numbered list, you can simply select the text and click the adjacent icons in the Paragraph pane of the Home tab. The type of bullet or number used will be linked to your theme, but you can select your own style from the drop-down arrow next to the icons (see some of the options opposite).

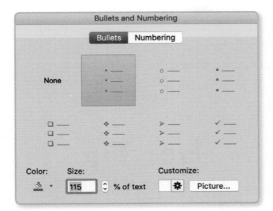

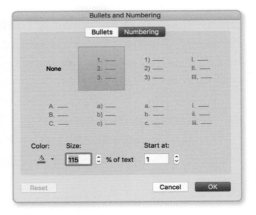

Above: Select the bullet options by highlighting your text and clicking on the adjacent icons in the Paragraph pane of the Home tab.

Above: You will find the numbered list options in the Paragraph pane in the Home tab.

Getting Fancy with Bullet Points and Numbered Lists

In order to customize the appearance of bullets and numbers even further, you can select the Bullets and Numbering option from the dropdown menu found in both icons within the Paragraph pane. Here you can choose emojis or even a picture.

Convert To SmartArt

PowerPoint also has a great built-in way to liven up your lists. Selecting the text for an entire slide will give you the opportunity to choose a number of coloured graphics that will present your list in a more pleasing manner. See more SmartArt tools on page 145.

Hot Tip

If you're continuing a numbered list from the preceding slide, change the 'Start at' number from within the Bullets and Numbering window. For example, if there are five points on a previous slide, the next slide should start with number six.

Other Basic Text Formatting Tools

The text formatting bar within the Home Ribbon tab contains a ton of options for text-tinkering. Before we move on, here are some more explanations of the basic formatting tools' functions.

➔ **Strikethrough**: To add a line through the middle of some text, select the text and hit the icon.

➔ **Change Case**: To turn a lower case word/sentence into upper case, or capitalize the first letter of each word in a title, use this drop-down menu.

➔ **Character Spacing**: This can be handy when trying to make text fit into a box.

➔ **Line Spacing**: This drop-down menu in the Paragraph section on the Home tab allows you to select the gap between the lines of text within a particular content placeholder. The default setting is 1.0; double-spacing, naturally, would be 2.0.

> ## Hot Tip
>
> **Hitting the 'Clear All Formatting' button in the Home tab will clear the various bolds, underlines or colours from your text.**

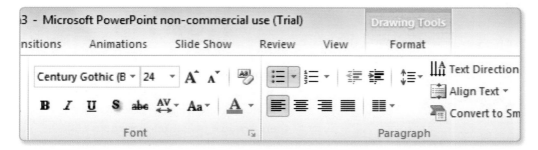

Above: There are many formatting functions available for text; all of these tools can be found in the text formatting bar in the Home tab.

FONTS

Fonts are the style in which your text is presented and there are literally thousands of them.

Changing Fonts

The easiest way to change the font of your text is to select the dropdown arrow from within the Ribbon. Hitting this will present the whole Fontbook available within Microsoft Office. If you choose one of these options while the relevant text is selected, it will instantly switch to the new font (PC only). To begin writing in a new font, make the selection when no text is selected and begin to type.

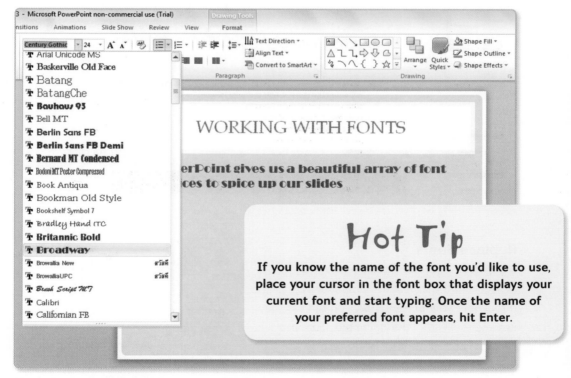

Hot Tip

If you know the name of the font you'd like to use, place your cursor in the font box that displays your current font and start typing. Once the name of your preferred font appears, hit Enter.

Above: There are almost countless fonts to choose from, all of which can be found in the drop-down menu in the Home tab.

Text Fonts in Themes

If you have selected a theme for your PowerPoint presentation (*see* page 52) then it will include some pre-selected font pairings that work well together. For example, the Angles theme (shown in the screenshot left) works well with Franklin Gothic Medium for titles and Franklin Gothic Book for body text. In order to borrow well-coordinated font pairings, hit the Fonts drop-down menu in the Design tab to choose (it sits below theme colours on the Mac), for example the Arial and Times New Roman.

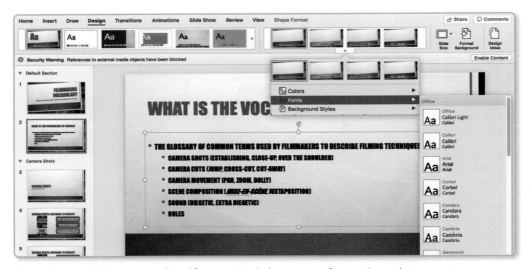

Above: Themes include some pre-selected font pairings, which you can use for your chosen design.

Replace Fonts

If you decide you want to abandon and replace a font that features prominently throughout your presentation, you can use the Replace tool within the Home tab. (Format > Replace Fonts on a Mac). Here you'll be presented with a dialogue box asking you to select a replacement from a drop-down menu.

Hot Tip

Like the colours within themes, these fonts have been chosen for a reason: they look good together. You're welcome to change them to your own combinations, but beware!

COLOURS

Earlier in this book, we likened the process of building a PowerPoint presentation to decorating and furnishing an empty house. Unless you're living within the set of a Stanley Kubrick film, it's hard to imagine taking residence in a house with white painted walls and white furniture, so let's add a splash of colour to liven things up a little.

CHANGING FONT COLOURS

The default PowerPoint text colour is, naturally, black, but there's an entire spectrum of colours at our disposal here. The easiest way of changing your font colour is to select the text and choose the drop-down arrow within the text formatting tools on the Home Ribbon tab, which presents the full range of options.

Choosing Font Colours to Suit Your Theme

The first option when selecting from the drop-down menu is to select a font from within your theme colours. This is a helpful tool, as it only presents options that will co-ordinate with the overall look and theme you've selected for your presentation. As you can see, there are various shades to choose from for each theme colour; simply hover over the colour of your choice and

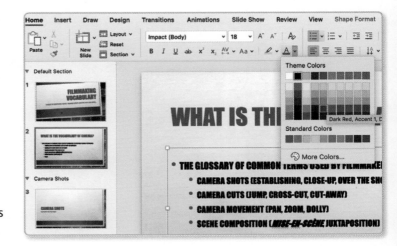

Above: The theme font colours list is great as it only gives you options that will co-ordinate with your selected theme.

click. If you've pre-selected the text you want to change, this will change the colour; otherwise, the next word you type will appear in the new hue.

Standard Colours

You're a rebel and you're not going to let Microsoft's highly-paid specialists inform your colour choice! As an alternative you can choose between the standard colours (the purest reds, blues, greens, etc.) that appear within the menu. Again, select the text first to change existing text.

The 'More Colors' Spectrum

The full rainbow of colours is available within this menu. You can drag your cursor around the wheel to select the most precise shade.

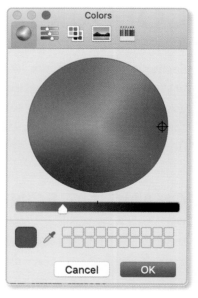

Above: The custom colour spectrum gives you complete control over your colour selection.

CHANGING THEME COLOURS

Once again, Microsoft's experts have put a lot of thought into selecting the colours for the various theme designs and served up a wide range of colour schemes that match (text, backgrounds, boxes, hyperlinks and various design elements). If you've chosen one theme but prefer a different

Above: You don't have to stick with the pre-selected colours of your chosen theme; you can select colourways from other themes to suit your presentation.

colour scheme select the Colors option from the Design tab within the Ribbon (Themes on Mac) and choose from the drop-down menu. You'll see the names of the other themes next to the colour palette they employ.

CHANGING BACKGROUND COLOURS

As previously hinted, each PowerPoint theme has pre-defined background styles that appear behind all the content but also match up with the other design elements. Think of them as the wallpaper behind the paintings you hang on the wall. Each theme has multiple styles , including solid colours and various gradient shading options (which neatly intersperse two or more colours).

Customizing Your Background Styles

The default PowerPoint Background Styles are attractive, but you can tailor them more to your own desires with the Format Background window within the Background buttons; here are some of the key options on offer.

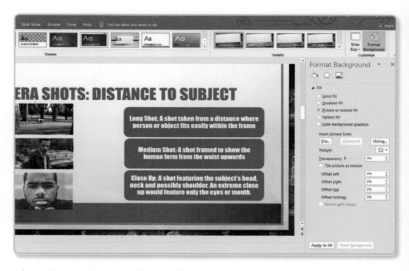

Above: You can alter the gradient shading options once you have selected your theme. This is easily done by the format background option in the Background Styles button and Format Background.

‣ **Solid fill:** Paints the background with a single solid colour.

‣ **Gradient fill:**
Allows you to customize the type, direction, colour, brightness and transparency of the gradient shading. Play with this and you'll get a feel for it.

➔ **Picture or texture fill**: Use this option to add a photo or pattern from your computer. Be careful, though: if there's too much going on within the frame, it'll be harder for your audience to see the important information clearly.

➔ **Pattern fill**: Choose from a number of pre-made patterns and adjust the colours. Again, this may make it more difficult to see your text, so use with care.

Hot Tip

For beginners and experienced users alike, it's best to stay within the background colours indicated by your theme to avoid nasty colour clashes.

Hot Tip

If you're unhappy with the custom changes you've made to a background, you can simply hit the Reset Slide Background button to return it to the original settings.

WORKING WITH WORDART

Once you're happy with your fonts, you can take it to the next level through Microsoft's WordArt Here you can furnish your words with a host of preset designs that add colour, outlines, gradient shading shadows and effects to your text, while still retaining your font. You can access the WordArt options through the Drawing Tools (PC) or Shape Format (Mac) tab,

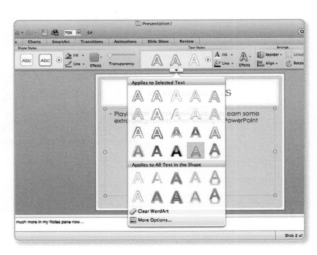

Above: WordArt styles provide an array of options that you can apply to individual words and letters or to everything within your placeholder.

which only appears in the Ribbon when working with text.

You can see three examples of the letter 'A' within the WordArt pane, but select the drop-down arrow to bring up the full array of text styles. You can choose to apply the text effects to everything within the content placeholder or just to the words you've highlighted.

Text Fill and Text Outline

You can further customize text styles by using the following commands, which are located next to the WordArt Styles pane in the Format tab.

- **Text Fill and Text Outline**: This will change the colour of the body of the text. You can select colours that match your theme or standard colours. If you'd just like an outline with no colour fill, select No Fill.

- **Text Fill**: This will change the colour of the body of the text. You can select colours that match your theme or standard colours. If you'd just like an outline with no colour fill, select No Fill.

- **Text Outline**: This will change the colour of the outline of the text. If you don't want a text outline, it's easy to select No Outline.

Hot Tip
Play around with the many WordArt styles by hovering over the various options within the drop-down menu and pressing click. This way, you'll see what looks good and bad on your slides (PC only).

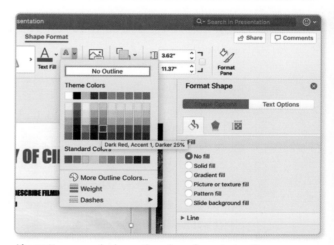

Above: You can easily change the colour of your text outline, providing a contrast with the fill or simply making it stand out..

Text Effects

These options, which appear within the Drawing pane of the Format tab in a drop-down menu beneath the Text Fill and Text Outline menus, take text design to the ultimate level.

➔ **Shadow:** Add a shadow beneath the text to suggest that light is shining on the words.

➔ **Reflection:** This option offers a slight reflection beneath the text.

➔ **Glow:** This effect gives the text a warm glowing outline.

➔ **Bevel:** A 3-D-like effect.

➔ **3-D Rotation:** Toggling these settings will alter the angle of the text in 3-D space.

Above: You can quickly and easily play with your text to transform its shape, shadow, reflection and glow!

➔ **Transform:** Completely alters the shape of the text. For example, it can form a semicircle, or it can be slanted up or down. Just hovering over the examples will show you how the effect will look on the slide (PC only).

Hot Tip

Rather than converting existing text to WordArt, you can insert a WordArt text box featuring your chosen text style. Hit the Insert tab (select Insert in top menu on Mac) and click the WordArt button; then click the style of your choice from the drop-down menu and a text box will appear in the centre of the slide with the default 'Your Text Here'. Overwrite it to add your own text in WordArt.

TRANSITIONS AND ANIMATIONS

We'll now move on to improving how your presentation looks when moving between information and between slides – transitions and animations are key to this.

TRANSITIONS

Transitions are attractive effects that can be employed to control how you move from slide to slide when you're delivering your presentation to an audience. They do not affect the information or how it appears within the slide but simply determine how one slide disappears and the next one appears. In order to access the Transitions control panel, you can select the dedicated Transitions tab within the PowerPoint Ribbon.

Types of Transition

Once you've selected the Transitions tab, you'll see the array of effects available to you. However, clicking the drop-down arrow will reveal the full extent, split into three categories.

➡ **Subtle:** Among these options are the more basic – but often most effective – transitions, such as Cut (jumps from one to the next) and Fade (adds a dissolve effect between slides).

➡ **Exciting:** Among the more elaborate transitions are the Honeycomb, Glitter and Vortex.

Hot Tip

In order to apply the transition settings you've chosen to the entire presentation, hit the 'Apply To All' button on the right of the Transitions tab.

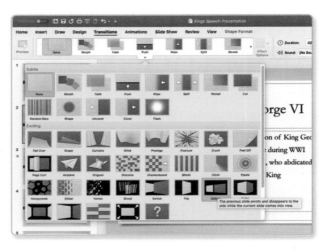

⊖ **Dynamic Content**: The text appears to land on the slide from a different location.

How to Add Transitions

Use Slide View on the left of the Window and select which slide you'd like to apply the transition to. Note that you will need to select the slide that will receive the transition, rather than the slide from which you'll be transitioning.

Above: The Transitions tab provides an array of effect options to get your presentation moving (quite literally!).

Then, from the Transitions tab within the Ribbon, click the effect of your choice to apply it automatically to the slide. PowerPoint will then show you a representation of how it looks; in order to see it again, click the Preview button on the left of the tab. If you decide to change the transition, simply click on another one from the menu, whereas to delete a transition, click the 'None' icon from the drop-down menu.

Transition Options

Apart from adding the transition, you can also customize the direction in which it moves, its duration, any audio effects you'd like to add and how to advance, whether you'd like a sound to play alongside the transition.

⊖ **Effect Options**: Here you can choose how the transition appears. For example, if you've selected the Shape option, you can choose whether the new slide transition appears as a square, diamond or circle and whether the shape moves in or out. Not all Transitions have variations. In these instances, the Effect Options button will be greyed out.

Duration: Adjusting the numbers within this box will alter how drawn out the transition is. You could build anticipation to a particular slide by making this 3–4 seconds long. Normally one second will suffice.

Sound: Here you can add stock sound effects to accompany the transition: a round of applause, perhaps? Want rid of the sound? Click No Sound within the drop-down menu.

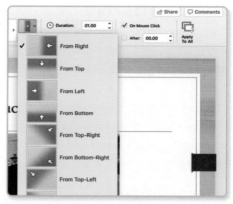

Above: Effect Options allow you to control transition timings, directions and sounds.

Previewing Your Transitions

Applying a transition will automatically show you a preview of how it will look. Just click the Preview button on the left of the Transitions tab to play it again or to test duration and sound effects.

Hot Tip

When a transition is applied, you'll also see a small box with an arrow next to the slide in Slide View or Slide Sorter View.

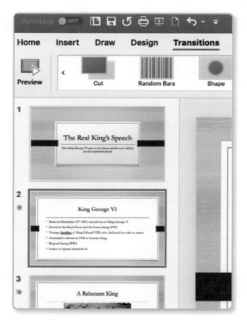

Above: The star symbol will appear next to your slide thumbnail once a transition has been applied.

ANIMATIONS

Animations can control how information enters, moves within and exits a PowerPoint slide, and multiple animations can be added to each content placeholder. Animations can be applied to any object within a slide, from singular pieces to entire blocks of information

They are especially important when you wish to reveal your points one at a time or would like them to appear in a certain order. Like transitions, animations are also a very useful tool in improving the overall look and feel of your presentation. Animations have their own tab within the Ribbon user interface and selecting this tab will present all of the options available to you.

Above: The Animations tab controls the movement of the information you have chosen to animate. The star symbols indicate what kinds of animations are available.

Applying an Animation

In order to choose an animation, start by clicking on the Animations tab in the PowerPoint Ribbon user interface and then select the content placeholder featuring the information you'd like to animate. Choose whether you want an Entrance, Emphasis or Exit animation from the drop-down menu and click it to apply. This will instantly launch a preview of the effect you've chosen.

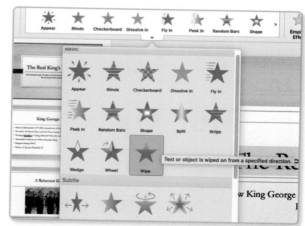

Right: The animation drop-down menu gives a vast range of options for the entrance, emphasis or exit of your information.

Hot Tip

If you want to apply the animation to a word/line/sentence of text, highlight it first, otherwise the animation will apply to the whole box.

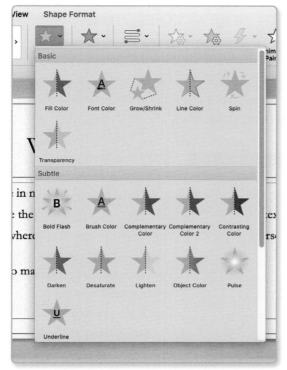

Above: The Emphasis effects are used to to draw attention to the selected object.

Types of Animation

Within the Animations tab, you'll see the star icons represent the various effects.

Pictured initially are the most commonly used tools, such as Appear (brings the text on screen with little fuss), Fly In, Fade and Wipe (bring the information in with slide design effects befitting their name). Selecting the drop-down arrow will reveal the full extent of the animations available and they are split into three 'E's:

- **Entrance**: These animations allow your words to Fly, Float, Bounce, Swivel and more. These effects are colour-coded in green.

- **Emphasis**: An emphasis effect can make your text or shape Pulse, Teeter, Spin and more. Emphasis effects are colour-coded in yellow.

- **Exit**: These animations perform the opposite action to the Entrance ones instead of Appear, you have Disappear and instead of Fly In, you have Fly Out. The Exit effects are presented in red.

Above: The animation painter tool turns your cursor into a paintbrush that allows you to quickly apply the same animation to other objects.

The Animation Painter Tool

Once you've added the animation, select then object and you'll see the Animation Painter button light up in the Advanced Animation Pane. Click it and your cursor will become a paintbrush; click within other placeholders to apply that animation to the new object.

Using Motion Path (PC)/ Path Animations (Mac)

We have listed this option outside of the three 'E's (Entrance, Emphasis, Exit) because the Motion Path/Path Animations can be tailored to act like all three. It creates a pre-set path along which the object (text, picture, etc.) moves within the slide. So, if the Path starts outside the slide and ends up within it, it's almost like an Entrance effect.

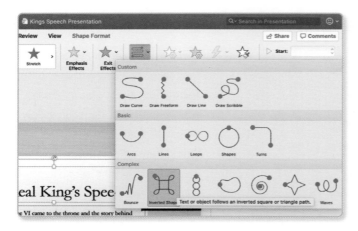

You'll see from the drop-down Animations menu within the Animation tab that Microsoft has kindly added some pre-set arcs, shapes, loops, lines and turns; select one to add it to your content placeholder. From there, you'll see a dotted line indicating the path along which the object will move.

Above: The Motion Path/Path Animation tool works to combine the three 'E's (Entrance, Emphasis, Exit). It creates a pre-set path for the animation, and there is a range of path shapes to choose from.

The green arrow represents the start and the red arrow represents the end of the path. We've selected the 'Arcs' tool, as you can see in the screenshot to the right.

These lines can be stretched/reversed or moved by clicking on them. In order to move the box to a new position, just grab it or use the markers to change its appearance. The effectiveness of Motion Paths can be quite hit-and-miss so it's best to play with them and see what you think looks good.

Above: If you want to be really original you can create a custom motion path, tailored to your presenting needs.

Drawing a Custom Path

If you're feeling up to it, you can write your own Paths Animations by using the Custom tool within the Motion Path/Path Animations tool. Here you'll see the opportunity to draw curves, lines, freeform or squiggles. Choosing a Custom Path will bring up the pen tool. Hold down your left mouse button and move the mouse/trackpad to draw. Double-click when you have finished and hit the Preview button to take a look.

Applying Multiple Animations

In most instances, one animation per point will do. However, if you're so inclined, you can add an entrance animation, an emphasis animation and an exit animation to a single piece of information to create a combination of stylish effects.

In order to showcase how this works, we'll concentrate on adding them to a Title placeholder. First of all, add an entrance effect (we'll go with Fly In). Once you've added this, you'll see a number 1 box appear next to the title content placeholder.

If you'd like to add a second effect (in our case the Pulse Emphasis), select from the drop-down menu in the centre of the screen. Once you've selected the Emphasis, you'll see a number 2 box appear beneath the number 1 box on the left of the slide. In order to add a number 3, and an Exit animation, repeat the previous step. Now you should have an Entrance, Emphasis and Exit animation. Each can be customized further in the Animation Pane.

Right: Applying multiple animations to one object isn't as tricky as it sounds. Each effect will show up on the left-hand edge of the slide so you can easily keep track of them.

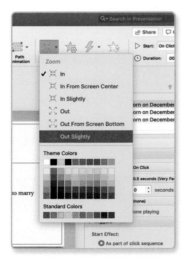

Above: Animation Effect Options give you complete control over the look and movement of your animation.

Using Effect Options

Just like the transitions we discussed previously, once you've selected an animation you can customize it further by using the Effect Options button. For example, if text is floating into a slide, you can use this tool to control whether it floats in from the top, bottom, left or right, or if you've selected Shapes from the Motion Paths animations, you'll be able to control exactly which shape you'd like to employ.

Hot Tip

When testing various animations, you can press the Preview button on the left of the Ribbon to see if you're happy with them.

Using Effect Options to Customize Sequences

If you apply an animation to a content placeholder, PowerPoint will automatically apply an individual animation to each bullet point, which means points will appear one at a time rather. You can change this setting in Effect Options from the Animations Ribbon tab and move down to Text Animations in the pane. This will allow you to select whether the animation appears As One Object, All at Once or By Paragraph, i.e. there's a click needed to progress to the next point.

Right: If you want information within one content placeholder to appear at different times you can use the Text Animations section of the Animations pane.

THE ANIMATION PANE

Things can get a little complicated when working with animations: they're heavily customizable, there's a lot going on and a lot to consider. Thankfully, the PowerPoint Animation Pane can help to keep everything manageable. It features the animations you've applied, the order in which they'll appear and the duration of the effect. When working with animations, it's wise to bring this up immediately; to do so, click the Animation Pane button within the Ribbon tab.

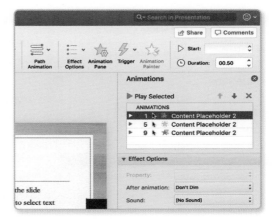

Above: The Advanced Animation Pane helps you to keep track of your animations and it's useful to always have this window open when working on animations.

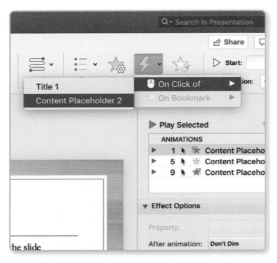

Above: The trigger tool allows you to select a certain area of the slide to act as a trigger for beginning an animation.

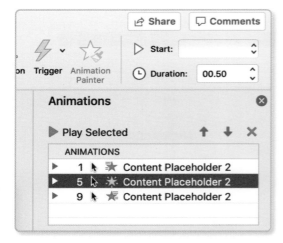

Above: The Animation pane allows you to grab your animations and drag them to the order in which you want them to appear.

Animation Triggers (PC only)

Once again, this is one of the more Advanced Animation settings; should you choose to, you can set up an effect to work when you click a certain area of the slide. This is useful if you reach a certain spot in your presentation where you want to add emphasis to a particular point. In order to activate it, click the Trigger lightning bolt and select the object you'd like to use as the trigger (usually a placeholder or picture).

Reordering Animations

When working within PowerPoint, we don't always add the effects in the order we want them to appear. The Animation Pane can rectify that: once you've completed the addition process, grab the individual animations with your mouse (hold down the left mouse button) and move them further up or down the list. You can also click the Reorder Animation buttons to move them up and down.

Animation Timings Pane

Although, for the most part, your animations will be activated by a click of the mouse or by hitting the down arrow on your keyboard during a presentation, if you're going hands-free, you can add some manual timings to your animations.

The Timings pane within the Animation tab controls when your animations start, how long they'll last and how long it takes for them to appear. These settings are called Start, Duration and Delay. From this portion of the user interface, you can also control in which order the animations appear.

Starting an Animation

Usually, an animation will commence when you use your favoured method to move to the next point (see pages 79 and 81). Selecting from the drop-down Start menu will allow you to customize these options, although it likely won't be necessary.

Controlling the Duration of an Animation

In order to adjust the speed at which your animation moves, select the animation of your choice from the Animation Pane or click the corresponding number box within the main slide. Then you can choose the Duration tab within the Timing box in the Ribbon (the default is 0.5 seconds).

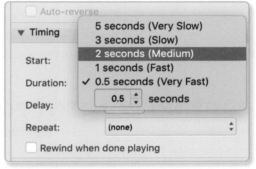

Above: The timings pane lets you control when your animations begin to appear and how long they will last for.

Above: The Animation Pane button also allows you to control the delay between several different animations.

Delaying an Animation

Within the Timing section you'll see the option to delay the start of the animation. For example, adding 1 second into the timing box next to 'Delay' will mean that there is a one-second gap between the end of one animation and the beginning of the next. You can see the timeline within the Animation Pane.

EDITING SLIDES

Before we move on to creating our own custom slides, here are some basic tips on editing the existing PowerPoint slide designs.

MOVING CONTENT PLACEHOLDERS

Most of the time, those placeholders within Slide Layouts are perfectly positioned and aligned for our needs, but it's quite simple to move the boxes. Firstly, click the placeholder of your choice, hover your mouse over one of the outlines until the pointer becomes a four-headed arrow, and then hold down the mouse button and drag it to the new position.

RESIZING CONTENT PLACEHOLDERS

If you'd like to make the placeholder larger or smaller within the slide, in order to add another item (see page 127), then hover your mouse over one of the square or circular dots at the edges of the box. The cursor will then transform into a two-headed arrow icon; from there you can drag the shape in or out to make it bigger or smaller.

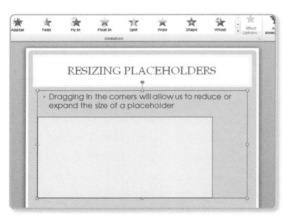

Above: It's very simple to resize your content placeholder to fit the design of each slide.

Hot Tip

Holding down Control while resizing keeps the centre of the object in the same place.

INSERTING NEW CONTENT

If you're looking to add new content placeholders to blank slides or those already populated by content, you'll need to create them. To do this, click the Insert tab in the Ribbon. Here you'll see the option to add Tables, Charts, SmartArt, Pictures and a Text Box, among others. While the first few will populate the slide for you, you need to draw your text box with the cursor by holding down the left mouse button and move the mouse/trackpad.

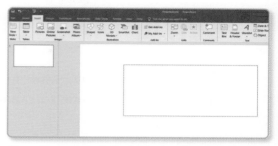

Above: Create content placeholders by selecting Content Placeholder from within the Text Box section of the Insert tab.

ADDING HEADERS AND FOOTERS

In order to add footers, you need to hit the Header & Footer button from the Insert tab in the Ribbon (Mac users select Insert Headers > Headers and Footers). This will summon a pop-up window offering date and time, slide number and text footer options. From here you can hit Apply to All or just Apply to add to the slide in question.

Above: You will find the Header & Footer button in the Insert tab. This will summon a pop-up window.

Headers and Footers in Notes and Handouts

You may notice the tab for Notes and Handouts within the pop-up Header and Footer window. All of the same options apply (page number, footer, date and time) but you can also add a header.

Above: Notes and Handouts also appear in the pop-up Header and Footer window. The same options apply but you can also add a header.

SLIDE MASTERS

Now that we're getting into the nitty-gritty of slide design and customization, it's time to call up the Slide Master tool and get creative.

WHAT IS A SLIDE MASTER?

A Slide Master, as the name suggests, is the key slide on which the others are based. So, if you modify the fonts, theme colour scheme, effects, backgrounds and placeholder sizes in the Slide Master then these changes will apply to each of the Slide Layouts (*see* page 61) within your theme.

Each presentation has a number of Slide Masters, whether you modify them or not, for all of the available slide designs. The Slide Master tool might seem a little intimidating, but it's actually incredibly helpful and can save you lots of time when designing a presentation, as it keeps a host of design elements consistent throughout without changing each and every slide. Let's dig in.

Above: The Slide Master tab tool can be found within the View tab in the Ribbon..

THE SLIDE MASTER VIEW

In order to access the Slide Master tab tool, select the Slide Master button within the View tab in the Ribbon. Once you've done this, you'll notice a new tab that wasn't there before on the far left of the window. Accessing the Slide Master tool changes the Slide View tool to showcase the Slide Master at the top, and underneath are thumbnails of each of the different Slide Layouts within a certain theme. You'll also see an entirely new set of formatting tools within the Ribbon, which will be described later in this section.

WHAT'S IN A SLIDE MASTER?

The Slide Master features a content placeholder for the Master title style and one for the Master text style, along with the various paragraph levels (*see* page 90). Beneath that you'll see the various slide layouts associated with that Theme. It'll also feature any design information from the theme and the background style associated with it. If you've added a header and footer then they will also be apparent within this slide.

EDITING YOUR SLIDE MASTER

Any changes you make to the Slide Master (which is the number one slide you'll see in the Slide Master view) will apply to the rest of the slides in the presentation *and* to those that you'll add to the presentation beyond that.

The process of editing the Slide Master is really no different to the changes we made to the fonts, format, colour and size when designing and editing the presentation in the first place. You can still use all of the shortcuts we mentioned earlier in the chapter (for example, Control+B, Control+U and

Above: There are lots of Theme options within Slide Master, allowing you to alter the setup of placeholders as well as colours, fonts and designs.

Hot Tip

It's a good idea to make the changes before adding all of the content to your remaining slides to ensure that nothing is knocked out of sync.

Adding Recurring Text and Objects to a Master Slide

You may want to add an item that appears in every slide throughout your presentation; perhaps you'd like to include a self-portrait, a shape, icon or a consistent text mantra you want your audience to take from the presentation. You can do this by selecting the Insert tab from the Ribbon and select Picture, Screenshot or a number of other options.

Hot Tip

Ensure you place the recurring object somewhere in the design where it won't interfere with the other information in the slide layout.

Adding Another Slide Master

It's possible to add more than one Slide Master to each PowerPoint project; this will give you the opportunity to create more custom design options for your presentation. Click Insert Slide Master from the Slide Master tab in the Ribbon

Control+Shift+>) and you can right-click or click the Insert tab to access the full text formatting panel. Once you're happy with your changes, you can select the Close Master View button to return to Normal View.

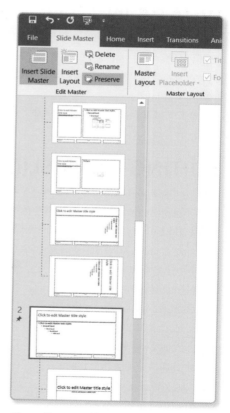

Above: You can add additional Slide Masters to your project, which can be saved and then selected from the Custom Design Option.

and this will add a clean Slide Master beneath the existing one, complete with each Slide Layout associated with that. Make your changes within this series and then return to Normal View. Now, next time you add a New Slide to a presentation you'll be able to select from the Custom Design option.

Hot Tip

When editing in Slide Master view, make sure that the Slide Master is selected rather than one of the layouts underneath, as changes to a Slide Layout will not be reflected in the Slide Master.

EDITING MASTER SLIDE LAYOUTS

At various points during this section we've mentioned that, as well as editing the Master Slide, you can also edit the individual Slide Layouts within a theme. Changes to text, titles and placeholders will not affect the whole presentation but will apply to that particular layout, each time you use it in your presentation. Each of the editing tools we mentioned in the Editing Slide Master section (*see* page 129) are also available to you when editing Master Slide Layouts.

Creating New Slide Layouts

Microsoft has done a fine job of creating the various Slide Layouts that are present within each of the PowerPoint themes. However, you can tear up the playbook and create your own to save and use consistently throughout your presentation. In order to enable this feature, hit View > Slide Master > Insert Layout.

This will summon a relatively blank canvas, featuring the

Hot Tip

If you make use of the Edit Theme pane while working within Master Slide Layouts then the whole presentation will be affected.

Above: Slide Master allows you to create and insert new custom layouts, which you can save and use throughout your presentation.

chosen theme design, a title content placeholder and the footers (both of which can be dispensed with by deselecting the boxes in the Master Layout pane). It will appear at the bottom of the Slide View pane but will populate the Current Slide view.

Click the Insert Placeholder drop-down menu within Master Layout in order to choose the style of placeholder you wish to add and then draw it in. You can also use the Insert tab to draw shapes (something described in more detail in the next chapter). Once you've finished perfecting your design, click Rename within the Edit Master pane to save it. After returning to Normal View (select Close Master) and hitting New Slide, you'll see this layout featured within the drop-down menu.

Saving Your Master Slides as a Custom Template

Way back in Chapter two we mentioned that when creating a presentation from a template (*see* page 55), there was a little section called My Templates (Personal on a Mac), reserved for your own creations. At that point we didn't have any, but now we do. In order to save your newly fashioned Slide Masters as a Custom Template, select Save As from the File tab, hit the drop-down menu, click on PowerPoint Template (.potx) and hit save. The saved template will now appear to you in My Templates in the New section of the Backstage View (PC).

CHANGING THE HANDOUT AND NOTES MASTERS

Earlier in the chapter we mentioned that there are at least three Masters for each PowerPoint presentation we create: beyond the Slide Masters you add, there are Notes and Handout Masters, which you can also tailor to your own needs.

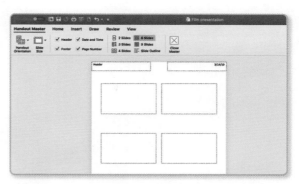

Above: Handout Master allows you to control the Page Setup, Handout Orientation, Slide orientation (PC only) and Slides Per Page and Placeholders.

Creating a Custom Handout Master

Select View and then Handout Master to summon the Handout Master tab. From this view you can tailor the Page Setup, Handout Orientation, Slide Orientation, Slides Per Page, as well as Placeholders like Header, Footer, Date and Page Number. There is, however, no opportunity to edit the size of the slides represented within the Handout view.

Above: You can customize the Notes Master to your needs, allowing you to amend the set-up and orientation of notes on your slides.

Creating a Custom Notes Master

Once again, hit View > Notes Master to access this page. From here you can amend the setup, orientation of the notes and the orientation of the slides appearing on the page (PC only). Additionally, you can customize what appears on the Notes page and change the sizes of the slide representation and the notes placeholder in the same way you'd alter the size of a content placeholder.

ADDING TO A PRESENTATION

ADDING IMAGES

Adding photographs is a great way to spice up your slide show, while PowerPoint is also a great tool for creating beautiful photo albums. In this section, we'll show you how to break up the tedium of text-based slides.

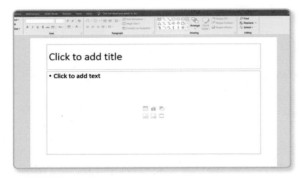

Above: Within each content placeholder there are icons indicating objects that you can insert.

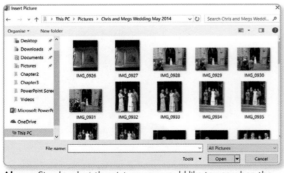

Above: Simply select the picture you would like to use when the box appears and press Open.

ADDING PICTURES

Helpfully, within every content placeholder, there are six icons that allow you to insert content (tables, charts, video, etc.). A couple of those buttons pertain to pictures. You can Insert from File or select Online Pictures (same icon with a globe). The former will enable you to browse your computer for available pictures, while Online Pictures will launch the ability to search images from Microsoft Bing.

Add Picture From File

Selecting the icon (bottom left in the Content Placeholder) will bring up a dialogue box. Find the picture that you'd like to use and press Open. The photo will now appear within the content placeholder.

Add Picture From Online Sources

The newest versions of PowerPoint handily offer access to online pictures. Clicking this button in the content placeholder brings up a new format tab with a range of categories. You can explore these or type a specific image in the search bar. Once you've found the image you want click 'Insert'.

Insert from Photo Browser (on Mac)

This brings up the Media pane and allows you to select images from your Apple Photos (Apple's photo storage app). Once you've found the image of your choice, drag it into the content placeholder.

Image rights

If you're using pictures sourced from online, you are responsible for respecting copyright. That's why there's a 'Creative Commons only' tick box when searching online pictures. These images are available to use freely. Using copyrighted images will likely be fine when presenting to a small group, like a classroom, but if you're using the presentation for commercial purposes you can only use images you have the rights to. Better safe than sorry here.

Design Ideas (Office 365 only)

If you're an Office 365 subscriber, PowerPoint will serve up some intelligent design ideas when you insert an image into a slide. These will show up in a format pane on the right of the display. These will show the image in different sizes and positions on the slide, and give you the opportunity to choose from a number of new layouts. This will save you some work.

Above: Design ideas can spruce up your slide with a professional look without you having to do any work at all.

Adding Pictures Outside of Content Boxes

If you'd like your picture to appear within a particular content placeholder, it's important to use the Insert tool within the placeholder or to select the placeholder before you use the Insert tool from the Ribbon. If you don't do this – or if you're using a blank slide layout – the photograph will just appear in the centre of the slide. If the photo you've chosen is larger than the confines of the slide, it will be scaled to fit.

Hot Tip

If you add an image to the Slide Master (see page 128), it will appear throughout the presentation in the same position on each slide.

Above: If you insert a picture within the content placeholder, which would otherwise be larger than the slide, it will be automatically scaled to fit.

Image File Formats

File formats are represented by the letters that appear after the dot in the file name (for example, .jpg, .tiff and .bmp). Since PowerPoint is such a universal tool, it'll play nicely with most formats.

ADDING CLIP ART

One way to avoid copyright complications is to use ClipArt. Sure, it won't look as nice, but it beats being chased down by an angry photographer. Microsoft has given us a sizeable library of stock images to kit out our PowerPoint presentations. These images and illustrations are called Clip Art.

Left: Clip Art has a great library of images that you can use to embellish your presentation.

Choose Online Pictures as explained above and then search for a picture (e.g. football). In Windows you'll see a drop-down menu for Type (on a Mac, select the Filter icon that looks like a funnel) and select ClipArt. Click the image of your choosing and press Insert.

Adding 3D Models

A relatively new feature in PowerPoint is the ability to add 3D Models. These images can be manipulated on a 360-degree axis and can add a little pizzazz to your presentation. You'll see an option to add these in the Insert Tab. On clicking the button a pane will appear to the right. You can search or select from categories like Emoji,

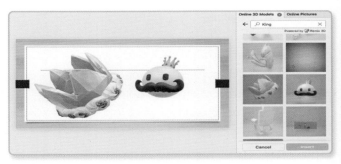

Above: Adding 3D Models is a recent addition to PowerPoint (PowerPoint 2019 and Office 365 only)

Animals, Avatars and more. Select your image and press insert. From here you can use the axis tool to reposition and rotate the photo however you wish.

Hot Tip

If you don't want to manually rotate your 3D Models, tap the image within the slide, hit Format and select the drop-down menu showing positioning options.

Adding Icons

There are a large array of symbols you can add to your presentation to illustrate your points. These sit in the Icons menu within the Insert Tab in the Ribbon. Access this, select the Jump to... drop-down menu to pick a category and then browse until you find the icon you want. Then press Insert to drop it into your presentation.

Adjusting the Size, Repositioning and Rotating Your Picture

Once you've added the picture, be it to a placeholder or to the slide itself, it's easy to resize, reposition and rotate it to your own specifications.

Resize to scale: To resize the picture and keep the scale, hold shift and click and drag one of the indicators at the edges of the photo.

Freeform resize: Use the square indicators across the top and bottom of the object to adjust height or width.

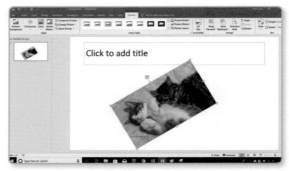

Above: Once you have selected and placed your image you can alter and adjust the size, position and rotation.

Repositioning: To move the photo elsewhere on your slide, select the picture and drag it to the preferred position within the slide.

Resize from centre: If you wish to keep your image centred, hold control when you drag the arrows at the edges

Rotating: You'll see a circle above the object with a curved arrow. Click and drag it clockwise or anticlockwise to rotate the picture. In order to rotate a picture in 90-degree increments, use the Rotate menu within the Arrange pane.

Changing the Size Using the Format Tab

If you want to get more precise, clicking on a picture will automatically summon the Picture Format tab in the Ribbon. Some of the options that appear within tab are as follows:

Shape height and shape width: Change the size of the picture by selecting the Size tab, clicking the up and down arrows in the height and width boxes. The aspect ratio is automatically locked so increasing the height will increase the width accordingly. On Macs make sure there's a tick in the Lock Aspect Ratio box in the Size panel. You can also type in the size of your choice.

Crop: Hitting the crop button in the Size pane will summon black borders at the corners of the picture. (Use these to select the exact area of the photo you'd like to use, and then hit the Crop button again to confirm.

Crop to Shape: Hit the drop-down menu on the Crop button to turn the shape into a circle, rectangle, a speech bubble or even an equation symbol. The picture will maintain its look but will be cropped within the shape.

Aspect Ratio: This tool crops the picture to fit the aspect ratio chosen.

Fill: Fill resizes the picture to fill the shape completely.

Fit: This option will show the entire photo within the dimensions of the placeholder, but it may not fill all areas.

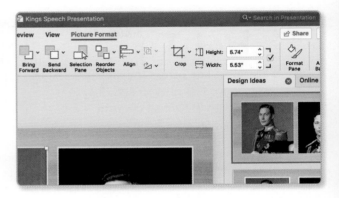

Above: The Format Tab allows you to customize the original image by changing the height and width, cropping, and adjusting the aspect ratio.

Hot Tip

In some instances, PowerPoint will not maintain the aspect ratio of your picture when dragging in the borders. To ensure that the proportions are maintained, hold the Shift key.

ADJUSTING AN IMAGE'S APPEARANCE

The Picture Tools Format tab lets you ditch the background in the picture, make contrast and brightness corrections, add a colour scheme and apply filters with Artistic Effects. Many of these tools apply to videos and audio so remember them for later on in the chapter.

Above: The Remove Background option will automatically remove the parts of the image that are not in the foreground; to be more precise you can manually select areas to delete and keep.

Above: The Corrections menu offers a large range of pre-set correction options.

Removing the Background

Clicking Remove Background will launch PowerPoint's attempt to leave only the foreground in place by highlighting the areas to be deleted in purple. To accept the changes hit the Keep Changes tick button, whereas to reject them, click Discard All Changes.

In order to keep or delete more areas of background, select the Mark Areas to Keep/Remove buttons and click around the edges of the photo you'd like to keep/remove. Hopefully when you're finished, you'll have a perfectly tailored image of a tiger with no background information.

Making Corrections to Images

The drop-down Corrections menu, within the Picture Tools Format tab, features a host of pre-set options for you to adjust the sharpness and softness and the brightness and contrast. Top left will decrease both by 40 per cent and bottom right will increase both by 40 per cent, while the centre thumbnail is neutral. To tailor these options more precisely, select the Picture Correction Options at the bottom of the drop-down menu.

Above: The Color menu contains options for saturation levels as well as complete recolouring.

Making Colour Changes

From the drop-down Color menu within the Picture Format tab you can alter the Color Saturation (Color Tone on Macs) from no colour to a 400 per cent colour boost and the Tone from low to high temperature, while also Recoloring the picture completely. Hover over the various options to preview.

You can also click the Set Transparent Color option and then click a colour within the image that'll be completely see-through. However, you can only select one colour to be transparent

Above: Artistic Effects can give your pictures that extra edge; choose from a pencil sketch or watercolour painting, amongst many others.

Adding Artistic Effects

Summon the drop-down Artistic Effects option to turn your photo into a pencil sketch or a painting, or to look like a watercolour painting or frosted glass window.

Reset or Change

Hit Change Picture to override the current snap from a file on your computer. Hit Reset Picture to delete all of the adjustments and effects you've made to a picture. Selecting the drop-down menu here will also allow you to reset any changes you've made to the size of the image and return it to its original state.

ADJUSTING THE STYLE

Click on the Picture Tools Format tab when working with an image you've added to a slide and you'll see the large Quick Styles pane packed with a bunch of framing options. Hover over these with a mouse to preview and click to select.

Picture Border and Picture Effect

These tools, within the Picture Styles pane, allow you to choose borders that adopt your theme's colours while the weight (i.e. thickness) of the border can also be determined from the menu. Selecting from Picture Effects is similar to the WordArt settings for enhancing text (*see* page 112). Here you can also add Shadow, Glow, Reflection or a different perspective on how the image appears in 3-D space.

Above: You can add a little depth to your slides by selecting effects such as the Beveled Oval for your images.

Picture Layout and SmartArt

Selecting from the drop-down Picture Layout menu also enables us to incorporate our pictures into SmartArt graphics. As we explained in Chapter one (*see* page 25), SmartArt turns pictures and words into design features that can break up endless bullet points.

In order to convert a picture to SmartArt, select a picture (click it) and hit Picture Layout from within the Picture Styles pane and select a diagram from the drop-down SmartArt menu. For example, your picture could represent a bullet point in a SmartArt list or a thumbnail image to illustrate a related point (see the images to the right for some examples). We'll talk more about integrating images within SmartArt later in this section.

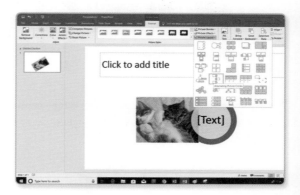

Above: The Picture Layout menu enables you to incorporate images into SmartArt graphics

ARRANGING TEXT, IMAGES AND OBJECTS

If you're combining multiple images and words (or video, charts and tables), you may need to adjust how they're arranged so that, for example, text isn't hidden behind pictures. Hit the Format tab for each content type (picture or text box). Here you'll have the option to bring forward, send backward, reorder objects or use the selection pane on the right of the screen to drag the items into the order of preference. Mac users have a great visual tool at their disposal (see 'Grouping Images or Objects' on page 146 when selecting reorder objects, and the screenshot to the right).

Above: The Selection Pane allows you to control the order of objects so that both your text and images are clearly visible.

Above: The Photo Browser for Mac enables you to select images from a variety of sources.

Hot Tip

Deselect the eye icons within the Selection pane to see how your slides look with or without the various elements.

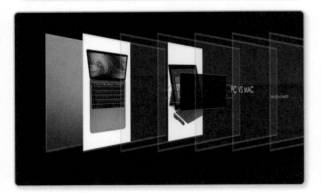

Above: The Reorder Objects screen for Mac allows you to drag items manually to the foreground and background.

Aligning Images or Objects

As with text-based placeholders, you can also anchor images to certain points of the page. Click an image and select the Align menu within the Arrange pane. Here you can snap the image to the left, right, centre, top, middle or bottom of the slide.

Grouping Images or Objects

Grouping together a series of images or objects (shapes, text, video, etc.) is useful, as it allows you to apply actions to them all at once (for example, rotating, flipping, moving or resizing). In order to group the objects, hold down the Control key and select each one; this should highlight them all. Then, in the Arrange Pane of the Format tab, hit Group. Images and objects can be grouped or ungrouped at any time.

Hot Tip

If you've been playing with the positioning of an image and want to bring it back to the exact centre of the slide, use Align > Align Centre.

PHOTO ALBUMS

One of the key uses for PowerPoint in the home is to create photo slide shows of family occasions. As we've discussed in Chapter one (*see* page 21), there are pre-set PowerPoint templates which make this easy. First you need to start a new presentation from a template (*see* page 53) to bring up the options. Simply search for 'photo album' to bring up the available options.

Hot Tip

When working with templates, don't use the Change Picture or Insert Picture options from the Ribbon to replace an existing photo in a placeholder. It may mess with the formatting of the template and the photos won't conform to the placeholder.

In order to add your own photos to the various placeholders, you must first delete the stock shots, which may be currently occupying the slots. Click on the picture and press backspace to reveal the 'Insert or Drag and Drop Your Photo' message. Click this to add a picture as you

Above: You can use a pre-set PowerPoint template to create an interactive photo album and slide show.

normally would, and it will conform to the size of the placeholder. Then use the image editing tools listed in this chapter to customize your photo. As the message suggests you can also simply click, hold and drag the photo from elsewhere on your PC and release when it's over the relevant placeholder.

Above: When working with a pre-set photo album template you can easily delete any stock photos currently occupying the slots. The wizard will create a series of slides from a folder on your computer featuring the photos of your choice in the style of your choice – and here's how.

POWERPOINT FOR PC PHOTO ALBUMS TOOL

PC users have a leg-up on Mac counterparts here, thanks to a photo album creation wizard, which doesn't involve working with templates.

1. Select Photo Album from the Insert Images pane and click 'New Photo Album' to launch the wizard.

2. Click File/Disk to choose the picture(s) from your computer, then select them all and press

Insert. All of the pictures are now listed in a numbered box, with a preview next door.

3. From here you can add captions to all pictures or make them black and white by selecting the respective tick boxes. If you want you can click to add a text box next to the picture of your choice.

Above: PowerPoint 2007 and 2010 for PC have a photo album creation tool that doesn't involve working from a template; use the Wizard to select a folder of images and go from there.

4. There are up/down arrows for moving pictures up and down in order of appearance; you can also remove individual pictures, use the rotate buttons and toggle with contrast and brightness.

The Album Layout section of the window allows you to determine how many pictures you'd like per page (the default is just one), the frame shape or even to pick from one of the PowerPoint themes. Once you're happy with everything, press Create and you'll have a quick and easy photo album. Now all you need to do is add text, titles and captions.

Hot Tip

Don't worry if you've missed out a picture; you can hit Photo Album > Edit Photo Album to add more snaps to your creation. To avoid having to do this, try to create a folder on your desktop featuring all of the pictures you'd like to use.

ADDING VIDEO AND AUDIO

Adding videos or audio from your computer or from the internet is a great way to add illuminating and entertaining content to your PowerPoint presentation – and it's just as easy as adding images. After explaining how to add audio and video separately, we'll talk about the playback and formatting tools together, as they're very similar.

ADDING VIDEO

If you're adding video from your computer's hard drive, select the video reel icon within a content placeholder. Simply locate the video of your choice from the pop-up dialogue box and click Insert. The video will fit to the content placeholder as best it can or appear in the centre of the slide. You'll now see a Video Tools tab appear in the Ribbon with two sub-tabs: Format and Playback.

Adding Online Video

PowerPoint makes it easy to add a video from online sharing sites YouTube and Vimeo to your presentation, putting millions upon millions of videos at your disposal. It's a perfect way to introduce relevant content into your presentation and add content. It's really simple to do, too.

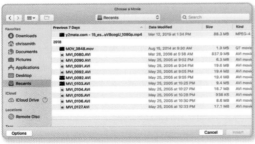

Above: Add a video by using the video reel icon within a content placeholder.

1. Go to YouTube.com or Vimeo.com and find the clip you'd like to insert. Copy the web link (URL) from the browser bar or the share options on that site.

2. Hit the Insert Tab and select Video > Online Video to bring up a dialogue box. Paste the video link into the box and press Insert. The clip will appear in your slide.

Video Browser on Mac

As with photos Mac users can insert video using the handy Media Browser. In order to summon this, select Video from the Insert Tab and select Movie Browser, which isolates compatible movie files. Once you've found the clip, just drag it into the slide.

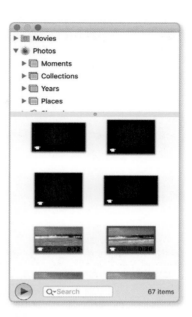

Hot Tip

If you're adding online videos, you'll need to have a connection to the internet when delivering your presentation. If this isn't going to be the case, you're better off using videos stored on your computer.

Above: For Mac users, locate the Media Browser from the Insert Movie button within the Insert Tab.

Compatible Video File Formats

There are hundreds of different video codecs in the world and not all of them will work with PowerPoint. The following will cover most videos you shoot on your smartphone, video camera or have downloaded from the internet:

PC:
Windows Video file (.asf)
Windows Video File (.avi)
MP4 Video File (.mp4, .m4v, .mov)
Movie File (.mpg or .mpeg)
Windows Media Video (.wmv)
Adobe Flash Media (.swf)

Mac:
AVI movie (.avi or .vfw)
MPEG-4 movie (.mp4, .mpg4)
Apple MPEG-4 movie (.m4v)
MPEG movie (.mpg, .mpeg, .mpe, .m75, .m15)
MPEG-2 video (.m2v)
MPEG-2 Transport Stream (.ts)
QuickTime movie (.mov or .qt)
DV movie (.dv or .dif)

ADD ANIMATED .GIF FILES

Animated .GIF files are a staple of the modern web. Essentially, they are short, looping segments of images/video that can add some colour to your presentation.

Right: Locate and copy the sharing code for your chosen video, from the online webpage.

Above: Under the Insert tab, click on video and select 'Online Video'. In the dialogue box you will need to enter the web URL.

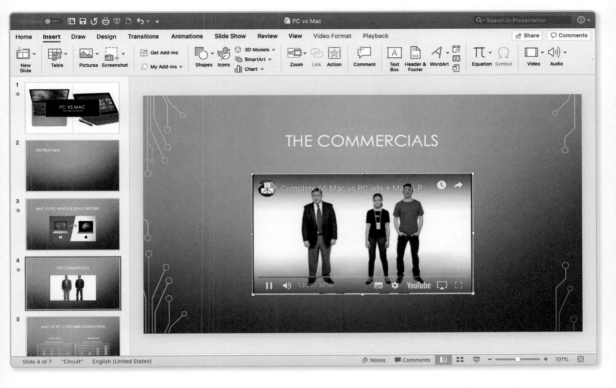

Above: Make sure you are connected to the internet when you give your presentation for the video to work!

From the Insert tab in the Ribbon, select Online Pictures. Here you can type in a search for 'animated gif' and choose from the options. If you're looking for something specific like the moon, type 'animated gif moon'.

Alternately, you can add animated .gif files in from your computer by inserting an image from file (*see* page 136), which is stored on your computer. The animation will only play when you're playing the slideshow.

AUDIO

In Chapter three (*see* page 117) we spoke of adding audio clips, such as a round of applause or a drum roll, to form a transition between slides, but the aural goodness in PowerPoint goes way beyond that. Here's how to add your favourite songs or sound effects to your slideshow.

Adding Audio to a Presentation

Click the Audio icon from the Insert tab to add a clip from File/From My PC. Select the clip of your choice from the pop-up dialogue box and hit Insert. It'll then appear within the slide, represented by a speaker icon and a playback menu that mirrors the video control panel explained in The On-slide Media Playback Controls (*see* page 156). Mac users can also use the Media Browser we mentioned on page 151 (Insert > Media > Audio Browser).

Hot Tip

Adding audio will be no use if you don't have speakers on the device you're using to playback the presentation.

Above: Add audio to your presentation by selecting the Audio icon from the Insert tab. This will enable you to select a track from your computer.

RECORD AUDIO

Newer versions of PowerPoint enable to record your own audio here using the built-in microphone on your PC. Perhaps a narration track for a particular slide? Select Audio from the Insert tab and choose Record Audio. Give your audio track a name and hit return. Once you've finished speaking, hit Stop. You can preview the file by hitting Play. If you're happy, select Insert and the file will appear within the slide layout.

Hot Tip

You can check the file format of your audio clip, video or photo by right-clicking the file and selecting Properties (Info on Mac).

Compatible Audio File Formats

You'll be able to add any audio file you've copied from a CD and most files that you've downloaded from online stores like iTunes, Amazon or more. In fact, there are very few audio files PowerPoint doesn't like. You'll be fine with all of these AIFF Audio file formats: aiff, .au, .mid, .midi, .mp3, .m4a, .mp4, .wav, .wma.

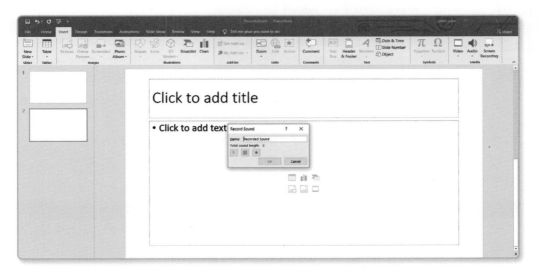

Above: If you want to record your own audio clip, you can use the internal microphone of your Mac or PC to do so. Simply select 'Record Audio' from the Insert Audio button.

ON-SLIDE MEDIA PLAYBACK CONTROLS

Whenever you add an audio or video clip, you'll see the media panel nestling beneath it. From here you can click the play button to start and stop (the space key also works), while using the rewind and forward options to browse through the clip at greater speed. The clock indicates how far you've progressed within the clip, while the speaker icon allows you to control the volume – just like the remote control on your home DVD player.

Above: The media controls allow you to start, stop, rewind and fast-forward your clip.

VIDEO AND AUDIO PLAYBACK TOOLS

Once you've added a clip from your computer, you'll see the Video/Audio Format and Video/Audio Playback tabs appear in the Ribbon. Select Playback to control the volume, and when (and from where) the clip starts, loops, fades, etc. If you've recorded a narration track or are using a piece of music to accompany your presentation, you can tick Play Across Slides to ensure it plays throughout. Many of these tools, like trimming the clip, are not available when selecting video from sites like YouTube.

Above: When you have added a media clip the playback tab will appear in Ribbon, allowing you to control volume, looping, etc.

Adding a Poster Frame (Video Only)

Rather than having an unattractive black box on your video slide, you can add an image to your video to appear as a placeholder before you press play. Click the Poster Frame menu in the Format tab and you'll see you can select an image from file; alternatively, you can pause the video at the most apt moment and then hit Poster Frame > Current Frame. When you arrive at the slide, this is the image you'll see.

Add a Bookmark

Adding a bookmark or multiple bookmarks to your media clip enables you to anchor text or other objects to appear at certain points, by using the Animations tool. To select a bookmark, hit play and when the video/audio reaches the point of your choice click the Add Bookmark within the Playback tab and a bubble will be added to the media progress meter.

Then select another object within the slide and hit the Animations pane. Add your animation, select the text and then hit the Trigger button. You can then select 'Bookmark 1' and the text will fly, float or appear on the screen at the precise moment of your choosing.

Above: You can add bookmarks in order to trigger animations, anchor text objects and more. To do this, play the media and hit the Add Bookmark button at the correct place within the media clip.

Trimming Your Video or Audio (Mac users, sorry, it's Office 365 only)

Once you've inserted the media file, hit Trim Video/Audio from within the Playback tab and you'll be presented with the window to the right. Play the clip and then pause where you'd like it to start and then drag the yellow marker to the time marker. Do the same with the red marker at the end portion of the clip and click Trim. You'll now see the newly trimmed clip within your slide. However, this can't be done with embedded video clips from YouTube or Vimeo.

Above: Use the Trim Video/Audio button in the Playback tab to select where you would like the clip to start and stop.

More Video and Audio Playback Options

The Audio/Video Playback tabs offer some more interesting tools for perfecting your use of media files:

- **Volume**: Controls the loudness of your clip.

- **Start**: Choose whether a click is required to start your video/audio or whether it'll begin automatically when it arrives on the slide.

- **Play Full Screen (video only)**: Selecting this will allow the video to take over the entire slide while it is playing. Great if you have no other information to show alongside it.

Hot Tip

To add a little professional polish to your video or audio clip, use the Fade In/Fade Out tool and set both timers in the Playback tab to 0.5 seconds.

⊖ **Loop until Stopped**: If you tick this box the clip will begin playing again from the start once it reaches the end. Press stop or hit the space bar to stop it. This is more useful for audio if you want the sound to play for the entire time that particular slide is displayed.

⊖ **Rewind after Playing**: Select this tick box if you plan on showing the clip more than once.

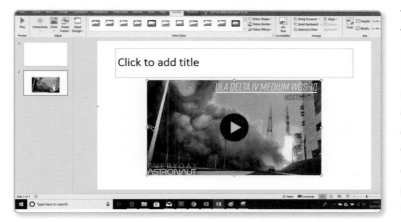

The Video Tools Format Tab

If you've added a movie from your computer you can edit it in the same way that you can edit a picture (see pages 139 to 145), i.e. you can make the same Corrections and Color changes, while

Above: Using the Video Tools Format Tab you can edit a video in the same way you can edit a picture; experiment with colour corrections, cropping, styles and effects.

you'll also have access to the same Crop tools, Styles, Borders and Effects. Essentially, the entire Video Format tab is much the same as the Picture Tools Format tab, so apply the same instructions listed earlier in the chapter to customize your video even further.

Formatting the Audio Clip

There's not much you'll need to do within the Audio Tools Format tab (Audio Format on Mac). There's no real need to alter the appearance of the speaker icon, which appears on the presentation. You may like to use the size arrows to increase the size or you may like to click the 'Hide During Show' tick box so the icon isn't visible on the slide, but aside from that, move along – nothing to see here.

TABLES

Tables are useful in PowerPoint presentations when you're seeking to present figures and information in an easily comparable format. If you run a local bowling league you can easy match up the names of players with the numbers of games played, wins, losses, strikes, gutterballs and points. If you're presenting the results of a poll, you can add the question and the proportion of recipients who selected each answer. Like most things within PowerPoint, tables are easy to create and can be richly designed and customized.

ADDING A TABLE

You can incorporate a table into an existing context placeholder by simply selecting Insert Table, i.e. the first of the six icons that appear there. You'll then be asked to select how many columns (vertical boxes) and rows (horizontal boxes) you'd like the table to include. If we use the bowling league analogy from above, we have five players and seven different headings for

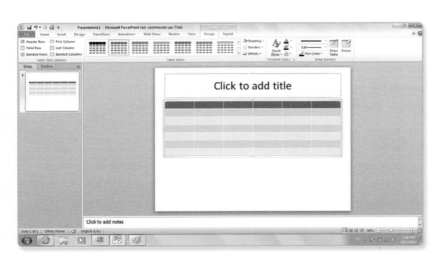

our information (names, games, points, strikes, etc.). That means we need a table with six columns and seven rows to fit everything in (see left).

Left: You can simply insert a table into an existing content placeholder and select how many rows and columns you'd like to include.

Alternatively, if you select Insert from the Ribbon and then hit Table, you can select a visual representation of the columns and rows you'll need. Hover over your preferred configuration with your mouse and click to insert the table into an existing slide.

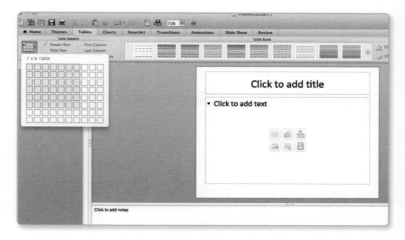

Above: If you select Insert table from the Ribbon rather than from within the content placeholder you can choose from a visual representation of the columns and rows you'll need.

Editing the Layout of Your Table

Once you've inserted your table, the layout is by no means set in stone. The Table Design and Layout tabs, which appear in the Ribbon whenever you're working on a table, allow you to alter its size and that of individual cells easily, while adding/deleting new rows and columns. Here are the most important commands.

Delete: Hit this to shed a row or column from the table.

Insert Above, Insert Below, Insert Left or Insert Right: These add rows/columns depending on where the cursor currently sits within the table. If you've selected, for example, three rows, Insert Below will add three more rows beneath the cursor.

Cell Size: Select a cell to adjust the size of an entire row or column by using the up and down height and width boxes arrow.

Distribute Rows and Distribute Columns: These buttons will undo any height and width edits and return the cells to an even spread across the table.

⊖ **Table Size:** To change table size, drag the corners of the table, but to more be precise, use the height/width arrows. Ticking the Lock Aspect Ratio box will ensure that everything stays within your pre-set proportions

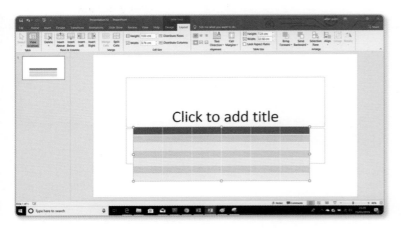

Above: The Table Layout will appear in Ribbon when you're working on your table and allow you to alter its shape and size.

Add Style

Once you're happy with the size, layout and content of your table, you can start adding a little panache. The default table style will always showcase colours that match your chosen theme, but you can change this with the Table Tools Design tab in the Ribbon, which appears when you're working on a table; here are some of the options.

⊖ **Header Row/First Column:** Highlights the top row in a darker shade. This can distinguish the information headings from the data.

⊖ **Total Row/Last Column:** If you're planning to add up scores in the bottom row or the last column then you can tick these boxes to draw attention to them.

⊖ **Banded Columns/Rows:** Ticking one of these boxes will apply alternate shades to each column or row – like a well-mown lawn.

⊖ **Table Styles:** As with pictures, videos and text, you can also add a little design panache to your table. Select the drop-down menu and choose from styles best matched to your theme, or from Light, Medium or Dark styles.

Shading: Select different shades from theme colours or standard colours. Keeping these relatively pale will make the information more visible.

Borders: These add physical lines around selected cells. To make the individual cells stand out you should either colour-band them (see screenshot below) or use borders.

Effects: Add a Bevel, Shadow or Reflection to the table. The latter is the neatest of these effects, whereas the Bevel effect feels a bit excessive.

Hot Tip

All text formatting tools are available to you when working within tables. These can be useful, for example, if you'd like to add bold emphasis to one or more pieces of information. You can also use the WordArt tools in the Table Tools Design tab.

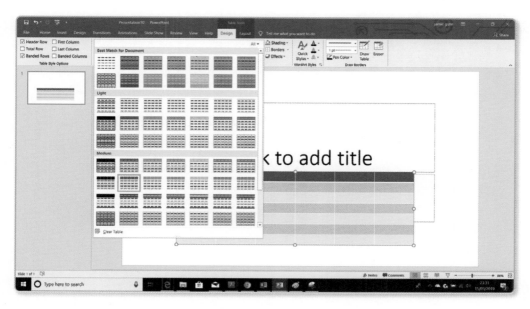

Above: Adding style to your table is very simple, just use the Design tools under the Table tools tab and start exploring your options.

Populating a New Table

You've erected your table – now comes the fun part: adding in all of the information. Just think of each box in the table as an independent text box. You can click within each one and what you type will be totally self-contained to that box. When you're done, press Tab to move to the next box or click wherever you'd like to add more info. As you can see below, our bowling league table is now complete.

Import Table from Excel

PowerPoint also enables you to import tables from Microsoft Excel, its spreadsheet creation platform that forms part of the Office suite. This already has a preset workbook for you to use. If you've created a spreadsheet, simply select them all (Control+A; Command+A on a Mac), hit Copy and them paste them into the PowerPoint slide of your choice. Here you can still use all of the layout and design tools, as well as the Design Ideas button (Office 365 only) to make it look pretty.

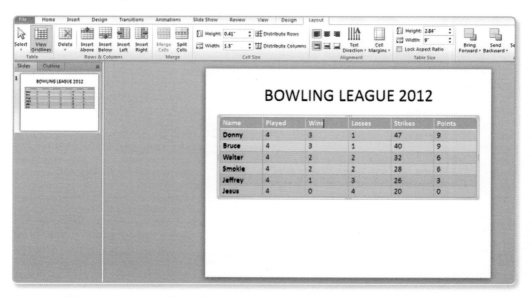

Above: To add information to your table, simply click each cell and type the information you would as in a normal text box.

CHARTS

Charts and graphs are the heartbeat of an information-heavy PowerPoint presentation. They're a fantastic, colourful and varied representation of data (sales figures, weather patterns, favourite ice cream flavours). Rather than simply looking at endless screens of numbers, charts can give an audience a visual perspective of your key points and arguments without making their eyes glaze over.

WHAT YOU'LL NEED

Before you start plotting your line graphs and bar graphs, you'll need a set of data: something to put along the x axis and something to put along the y axis.

TYPES OF CHART

Once you begin the process of adding a chart, you'll be asked to pick a type – here are some of the options you'll see under the various headings:

- **Column:** Data is presented in vertical columns, while categories (days of the week, months, ice cream flavours, etc.) sit along the horizontal x axis.

- **Line:** These graphs plot data points across the horizontal X-axis. Data points are joined by a straight line.

- **Pie:** Perfect for showing proportional data, as the size of the slice will depend on the percentage of the data each category represents.

- **Bar:** A Column chart that somebody tipped on its side. Numbers will appear to stretch for the finish line rather than reach for the sky.

Area: These are used to emphasize trends over time, e.g. if the rainfall has tripled compared to last year.

X Y (Scatter): These graphs combine two sets of numeric data and mark the point where they would meet if a line was drawn from both axes. For example, if you'd like to see how rainfall relates to air temperature.

Stock: If market wheeling and dealing is your game, these charts can be used to plot the opening and closing numbers as well as the high and low points on any given day.

Surface: These charts take the appearance of a topographical map; a surface chart colour co-ordinates numbers within the same range. For example, 0–2 would be in blue, 2–4 would be in red and 4–6 would be in green.

Doughnut: A pie chart that someone ate the middle out of.

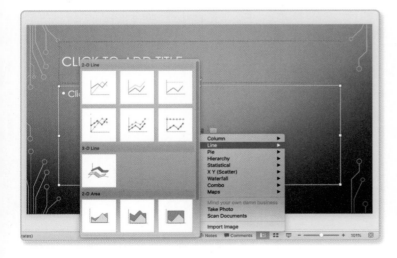

Above: The charts menu offers you a range of chart types to choose from.

Bubble: These are similar to scatter charts, but the size of the bubble accounts for a third set of data: the x and y axes could plot temperature and rainfall data, whereas the size of the bubble would represent the wind speed.

Radar: Rather than using the X and Y axes, a Radar chart anchors its data from a central point.

Each of these chart types has many different incarnations. For example, a column chart can place the data side by side or stack the numbers into one column; you'll see the different styles underneath different headings.

ADDING A CHART

Click the Insert Chart icon from within a content placeholder to summon a pop-up menu where you'll be asked to choose a chart type, such as those listed above.

Consider which is best for the data you plan to use, click it and hit OK. Alternatively, you can use the Insert Tab and simply select Chart. This can be a better options as it makes the best use of the space in the content placeholder. Adding a chart to a slide outside of a placeholder just pastes it over existing content – but don't worry, you can still move and resize to your exact specs using the methods we've become accustomed to.

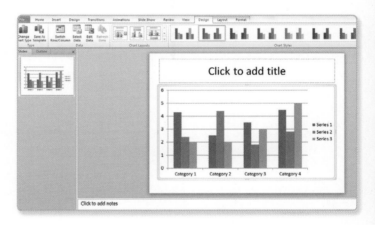

Above: You can insert a chart from within a content placeholder by clicking on the chart icon; this will summon a pop-up menu.

WORKING WITH EXCEL

When you choose a chart from the methods listed above, PowerPoint will call on the assistance of its partner, Excel. The number-crunching Microsoft Office stablemate will automatically launch. Depending on which version you're using, Excel may automatically and snap against PowerPoint so both programs appear together on the screen. If not, you can adjust the window sizes to make it so.

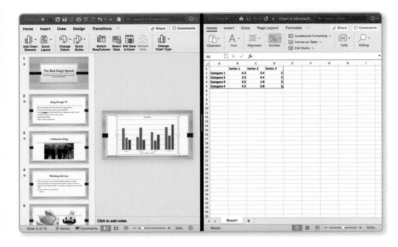

Above: Once you have chosen a chart, PowerPoint will summon Excel so that you can enter your data.

You'll see a default Excel document, called a datasheet, which supplies the information needed to populate the new chart you'll currently see on your screen. These placeholder numbers are just random series to give you a visual representation of how the chart will look.

Adding Your Own Data in Excel

Once the allied forces of PowerPoint and Excel are dominating your screen, we'll need to alter the data to our own. Editing these spreadsheets is the same as working within a PowerPoint table.

1. You'll initially see a list of four categories and three series of data. You can resize chart data range by dragging the blue marker in or out; this will add more, or delete, columns and rows to the chart.

2. We want enough room for seven days in the Category axis and three ice cream flavours in the Series value axis to chart our weekly sales.

3. Next, you need to change the names of your headings from Category 1, 2, etc. to the days of the week and then change the Series headings to add the names of the ice cream flavours we're flogging. Just click in the relevant cell and overtype the existing data, and then add your numbers. We sold seven strawberry ice creams on Monday, so add that number where the two axes meet.

4. Updates to the numbers will immediately be reflected in a change to the chart within PowerPoint, which we think is thoroughly awesome.

Changing Your PowerPoint Chart

If the chart you've selected doesn't quite offer the perfect visual representation of data you'd hoped for, it's easy to try a different option rather than deleting and starting from scratch. Just select the chart and you'll see the new Chart Design tab in the Ribbon. From this, select the Change Chart Type button and you'll be presented with the same options as if you were adding a chart from scratch – and all your data will remain intact.

Hot Tip

Excel also features a chart creation tool, so if you have an existing chart from that program that you'd like to copy to your PowerPoint slides, just copy and paste it (select Control+C to copy and then Control+P to paste in PowerPoint (PC) or select Command+C and Command+P (Mac)).

Tweaking the Design

The Chart Design tab features a host of tools that allow you to tweak the appearance of your chart and further refine which data appears and how that data is presented. You'll see this tab emerge within the Ribbon when working with charts.

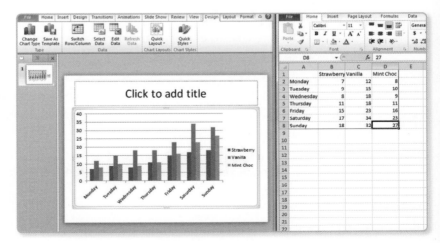

Above: If your chart does not look how you would like it to after the data has been entered, you can easily play around with chart types under the Change Chart Type button.

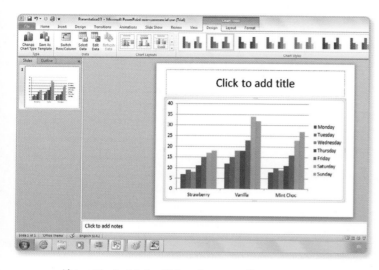

Above: The Switch Row/Column button quickly applies the data to the opposite axis..

Switch Row/Column (Switch Plot on Mac)

This simple button lets you apply your data to the opposite axis. In our case, pressing this button means that the days of the week now appear in the y (vertical) axis, while the ice cream flavours reside within the x axis. Sometimes this can alter the visual perception of a chart; for instance, now the focus is more on the pattern of ice cream flavours rather than the sales each day.

Selecting, Editing and Refreshing Data

The three other buttons under the Design tab allow you to tweak which figures are translated from the Excel datasheet to the PowerPoint chart.

- **Select Data:** Clicking this will summon a dialogue box from Excel. This can be used to tailor the range of data that appears within the chart. You can also add/edit labels to appear in the Legend.

- **Edit Data:** Hitting this button just sends you back to Excel to make any changes to the datasheet.

- **Refresh Data:** If you do end up changing the datasheet in Excel, the changes you make should automatically carry over to your chart. However, hitting this button will ensure your chart is updated with the most recent data.

Changing the Layout

Finding the perfect chart for your presentation is a three-step process. Firstly, you pick the type of chart (Column, Bar, Pie, Scatter, etc.) and then you pick from the list of variables (clustered, stacked, 3-D, etc.); remember you will have taken the first two steps when adding your chart.

The Quick Layouts button in the Chart Tools Design tab allows you to take the third step. As if those initial two choices weren't difficult enough, each chart type usually has around ten different layouts to choose from. These are minor changes involving where the legend sits on the page, whether numbers are written on the columns and whether a data table also features on the chart.

Chart Styles

Wait! Just when you thought you were done, there's a fourth step.

Above: The Select Data button allows you to control which figures are translated from the Excel datasheet to the chart in PowerPoint.

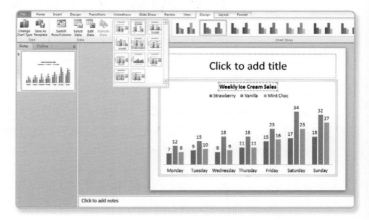

Above: After you have selected your chart style you can adjust the layout; simply choose from the options within the Chart Layout button in the Chart Tools Design tab.

You can also select from the PowerPoint Styles drop-down menu featuring a number of different style colour combinations for your chart. Some options place a background behind your chart, which can sometimes make for easier reading.

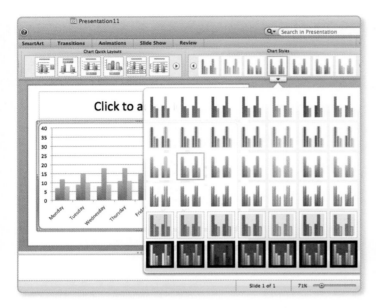

Above: There are also lots of pre-selected colour combinations for your chart to choose from!

Chart Colours

Your chart will adhere to the colours selected in your theme, but you can shake this up by selecting Change Colors from the Chart Design tab. Here you can choose from a wide range of colour schemes.

Add Elements to your chart

The farthest left option in the Chart Design tools reads Add Chart Element. This allows you to customize titles, axis names, legends, data tablets and more. Here are some of the options.

Adding Titles, Legends, Labels and Data Tables

The Labels pane within the Layout tab is a really handy feature (Chart Layout on Mac). Here you can add a host of important data to make your chart clearer to the audience.

↩ **Chart Title:** Use the drop-down menu to give your chart a name. In our case it's 'Weekly Ice Cream Sales'. Once you've selected the option, you can write it in on the slide.

Axis Titles: This can be handy in pinpointing what your x and y axes represent. Our x axis title is '6–11 August' and our y axis is 'Most Popular Flavours'.

↩ **Legend:** Most graphs come with a legend to illustrate which colours correspond to which data. However, this can be turned off or moved around using this button.

Data Labels: Most charts offer a visual representation of the comparisons without always reflecting exact numbers. Data labels can add these numbers into the chart and this tool allows you to position them accordingly.

Data Table: Most of the time we use charts so we don't have to make our audiences study boring oceans of numbers. However, if you want to supplement the chart with a data table underneath then be our guest.

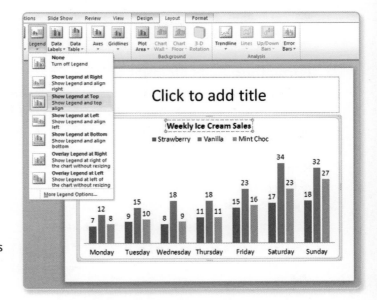

Above: The Labels pane is great for adding info that will make your chart clearer for your audience, such as titles and labels.

PowerPoint Chart Analysis Tools

Here are a few tools to key your audience in on what's going on within your charts. They can also be selected from the Add Chart Element drop-down menu.

Error Bars: Within the Analysis pane you can add Error Bars, which could reflect the margin for potential error, as they do with political polls.

Up/Down Bars: If you're working with a line chart, for example, you can use these to add bars marking the gaps between the sets of data.

Lines: By selecting the Lines option, PowerPoint draws a line from the plotted point on the graph to the bottom of the x-axis (almost a combination of a line and a column chart).

Trendline: These can reflect an average or even offer projections based on your data. Adding a trendline adds the data to your legend.

Formatting Each Element of Your Chart

Sometimes the level of detail in PowerPoint gets a little intimidating and this is one of those occasions. You can even format the Border Colours and Border Style. These options sit within the Chart Tools Format tab on the Ribbon, which is available when working with Charts.

Here you can select each individual element of a chart and use familiar formatting tools in order to further customize the look and feel of your table. For example, you can choose the bars in the chart and select colours, Styles, Outlines, and Shape Effects for each element. If you think it's too much, hit the Reset to Match Style button.

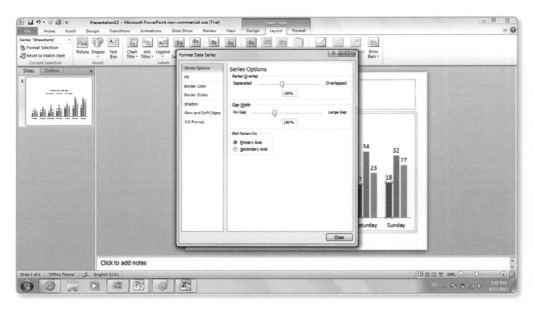

Above: If the amount of data and formatting options are becoming confusing, the Chart Tools Format Layout tab is really useful for working on individual parts of your chart.

SMARTART

SmartArt is labelled as such because it's, well, pretty smart and quite arty. It aims to convert those endless slides of text-based information into visually appealing graphical designs featuring colourful shapes, logical progression points and sometimes photographs too.

TYPES OF SMARTART

Before we go about creating our SmartArt diagrams, let's introduce you to what's on offer and how the different categories can work for your presentation. Hit the Insert tab and then click the SmartArt button to bring up the options, or you can select SmartArt from an existing content placeholder.

- **List:** Livens up your bullet points and secondary points with neat design features, while some selections can also represent information that runs in a sequence.

- **Process:** Highlights a logical flow of information,

- **Cycle:** Shows a sequence of stages, ideas that that spring from a central theme or interrelated ideas.

- **Hierarchy:** Allows you to choose a key point of information and feature the offshoots underneath. It could be great for a family tree or a chain of command.

- **Relationship:** Great for showcasing interlocking points like target lists, overlapping concepts like Venn diagrams or opposing ideas like pluses and minuses.

- **Matrix:** These show related points in four quadrants.

⊕ **Pyramid**: Showcasing hierarchical relationships between the many and the few (accessed by the Other button on Mac).

⊕ **Picture**: A host of options that incorporate photos. For example, a photo of a tiger could lead into a list of numbers left in the wild.

Hot Tip

Each of these SmartArt categories has multiple styles within it. Hover over a thumbnail for a detailed explanation of where it could be useful and which elements of your text will be included (primary and secondary, or just primary). This will help you to decide which diagram is best for your information.

ADDING A SMARTART DIAGRAM

Although it's possible to add a SmartArt diagram and then populate it with pictures and text, we'd advise that you build the bullet-pointed or numbered lists before you

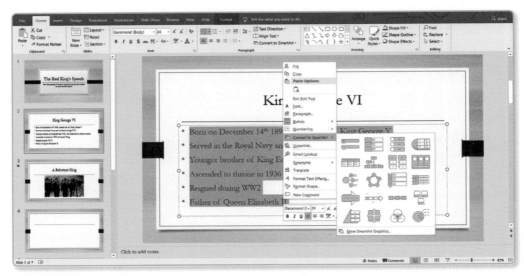

Above: There are lots of SmartArt options to transform your data. Browse these choices by simply hitting the SmartArt button in the Insert tab..

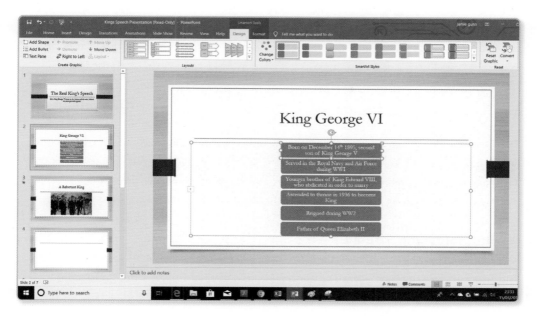

Above: Using the Convert to SmartArt tool is really simple as you can enter your information and then convert it to a SmartArt diagram.

start and then use the Convert to SmartArt tool. As you've probably seen from examining the types of SmartArt available, the tool plays nicely with primary and secondary text information.

Primary information is your key points, while secondary information is the sub-points; these are usually represented by a dash and are indented beneath the bullet.

Once you've selected the text (*see* page 105) you'd like to convert, identify the Convert To SmartArt button in the Home tab. From here you'll be presented with some common options. Hover over them with your cursor and you'll instantly see a representation of how your information will look in that style (PC only). If you see one you like, click on it. It's possible to change them at any time by using the SmartArt design tab.

Editing Text in SmartArt

You may have found the perfect 'Counterbalance arrows' design to represent the pluses and minuses of moving to a new city, but you still want to make some changes to the text.

You can click the diagram itself and edit text within the slide, but that's a bit fiddly.

The Text Pane, which can be summoned with an arrow in the top left of the SmartArt window, brings up a helpful Outline View style to look at your text. It can also be summoned by clicking Text Pane within the SmartArt Tools Design tab. You can also add bullets, promote and demote paragraphs or move them up and down using the Create Graphic pane within the same tab.

Adding Finishing Touches

As with everything in PowerPoint, there's always something you can tweak and polish. The SmartArt tool is no different and allows you to add all of the neat design touches, effects and styles we've come to know and love with other PowerPoint objects. They are accessible from the SmartArt Design and Format tabs, which pop into the Ribbon up when working with SmartArt.

Above: The Design Tools tab lets you make all the usual tweaks and changes to your SmartArt.

As you can see, you can select alternate layouts, and change the colour scheme of the SmartArt (the default colours match your theme) and SmartArt Styles, if you'd like to get a little 3D action going. The adjacent Format tab features all of the regular Shape Styles, WordArt Styles, Size and alignment tools. also, all shapes added through SmartArt can be resized, rotated and relocated like any other objects within PowerPoint.

EQUATIONS

PowerPoint is well equipped to cope with the needs of scientists and mathematicians, who want to present their work via a slideshow, thanks to the Equation feature. This gives you a host of common equations to choose from and all of the symbols and formula structures required to build your own. Non-scientific minds can look away now.

ADDING EQUATIONS (PC ONLY)

Within the Insert tab of the Ribbon, you'll see a nice large Equation button. Hit the dropdown arrow to see a host of commonly used equations (Pythagorean Theorem, Binominal Theorem and more).

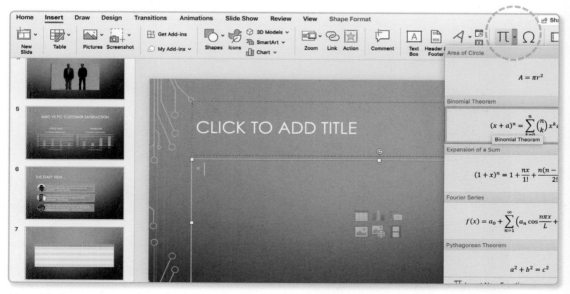

Above: The Equation button is located within the Insert tab in Ribbon. From there you will find commonly used equations.

However, if you select Insert New Equation at the bottom of the menu or the Equation button itself, you'll be transported to a new tab dedicated to equations.

Within the content placeholder, you'll see highlighted text that says 'Type equation here'. Within this menu, you can insert your own symbols by clicking the appropriate one within the Symbols pane of the tab. You can do the same with the various formula tools you'll see under the Structures pane. Each Fraction structure, Script structure, etc. has various options you can select from the drop-down menu. Once the structure is within your presentation, you'll see spaces for numbers and letters represented by small boxes with dotted lines. Click within these to overwrite with your own data.

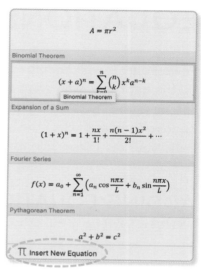

$$A = \pi r^2$$

Binomial Theorem

$$(x + a)^n = \sum_{k=0}^{n} \binom{n}{k} x^k a^{n-k}$$

Binomial Theorem

Expansion of a Sum

$$(1 + x)^n = 1 + \frac{nx}{1!} + \frac{n(n-1)x^2}{2!} + \cdots$$

Fourier Series

$$f(x) = a_0 + \sum_{n=1}^{\infty} \left(a_n \cos \frac{n\pi x}{L} + b_n \sin \frac{n\pi x}{L} \right)$$

Pythagorean Theorem

$$a^2 + b^2 = c^2$$

π Insert New Equation

Above: The Insert New Equation button.

DRAWING SHAPES AND OBJECTS

While SmartArt offers a huge array of pre-set, fabulously designed graphics to spice up your information, if you fancy yourself as a bit of an artist, there's also a host of pre-set drawing tools you can use to annotate your slides. You can use shapes as design tools to connect information.

DRAWING SIMPLE SHAPES

In order to add shapes to your slides, click the Insert tab and select the Shapes button drop-down menu of options. Once you've selected your shape, you can point your cursor back to your slide. As soon as you hold down the left mouse button or trackpad and begin moving the mouse, you'll start drawing. Drag the cursor out and the shape will be created before your eyes. When it reaches the size and proportions (height to width) of your choice, you can take your finger off the mouse button. The shape will be fitted with a colour to match your theme but, of course, this can be changed.

Types of Shapes

Selecting the drop-down Shapes button presents you with a staggering array of available shapes Here are the options:

Right: Select the Shapes button under the Insert tab (PC) and choose your style. Then simply hold down the left mouse button and start drawing.

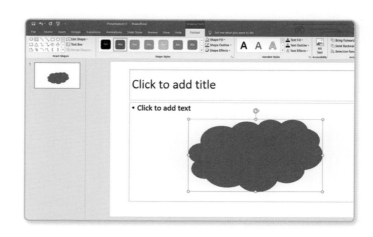

⊖ **Recently Used Shapes**: Here you'll see the shapes you've recently used.

⊖ **Lines**: A great way to link information within your slides. There's also a host of arrow connectors, straight and curved lines. When drawing curved lines, you'll need to click at the point where you'd like the line to curve and continue drawing.

⊖ **Rectangles**: Most commonly used for adding text. You can also draw shapes with one or more corners cut off, for a more unique feel.

⊖ **Basic Shapes**: Here you can add a host of commonly used shapes, such as circles and triangles, but also objects like smiley faces, weather symbols, 3-D cubes and more.

⊖ **Block Arrows**: Helping you to connect information with four-way arrows, arced arrows and more.

⊖ **Equation Shapes**: Add a plus, minus, divide by, multiply and equal sign, among others.

⊖ **Flowchart**: SmartArt does a decent job of creating flowchart-like objects, but you can design your own with this series of shapes

Hot Tip

If you want your shape to appear on every slide within your presentation, draw it on the Master Slide. For Master Slide tips head to page 128.

Above: There is a huge range of available shapes, just browse through the drop-down menu.

and some help from some of the above (lines, arrows, equations, etc.).

 **Stars and Banners**: Useful shapes.

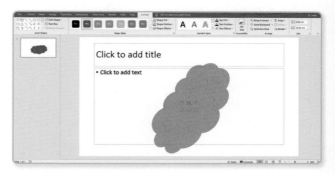 **Callouts**: Customizable speech bubbles which you can easily add text to.

Action Buttons: For use with clickable slides (*see page 190*). You can draw a play button, add a link and an action to it, and your media clip will then play.

Customizing Your Shapes

As we discussed when creating a text box (*see page 58*), you can resize, move and rotate a shape using the on-screen tools. Dragging the Sizing handle (white bubble) allows you to control the size, while clicking anywhere within the shape lets you drag it to a new position. Clicking the Rotation handle will allow you to drag-to-rotate, but you can also use the Rotate button in the Shape Format pop-up to rotate more precisely.

Adding Style to Your Shapes

In order to avoid repeating ourselves, we won't go into too much detail here, but

Hot Tip

Once you've drawn your shape, use the Control handle (yellow indicator) to customize the proportions. For example, if you've drawn a star, move the control handle in and out to determine the size and depth of its points.

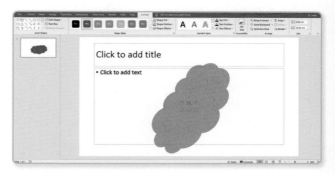

Above: Once you have chosen your shape you can alter its size, rotation and position using the on-screen tools.

Above: There are lots of options for changing your shape using the Drawing Tools Format tab.

within the Shape Format Tab, you can choose from the drop-down menus of Shape Styles, Shape Effects (e.g. Bevel, Shadow, Reflection and 3-D), Shape Fill and Shape Outline as we have throughout this book.

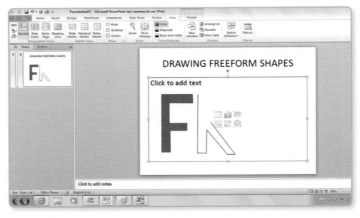

Above: The combinations of shapes and styles are almost limitless!

Drawing Freehand

Within the Insert Shapes menu, you can select the Freeform tool from the Lines section or Lines. This will turn your cursor into a pen tool and allow you to start drawing on your slide.

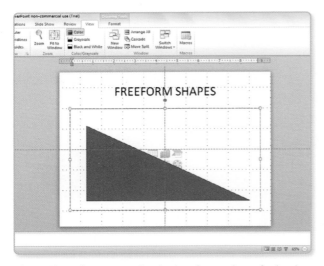

Above: The gridlines come in handy when drawing shapes freehand.

Drawing Freeform Shapes

The Freeform Line tool comes in really handy when creating your own shapes. After selecting the tool (Insert > Shapes > Lines > Freeform), click once at your start point, then release the mouse and move to draw a straight line. Click again when you'd like to form a corner and continue. If you'd like to go completely freehand at any point during this process, just hold down the mouse button.

Again, when you've finished drawing the shape, return to your start point and click.

Drawing on your presentation

If you have a PC with a touch-sensitive screen then the Draw tab in the Ribbon in PowerPoint 2019 and Office 2019 (as well as the mobile apps for Android and iOS tablet) is something you'll definitely want to explore. Otherwise it's much harder to make this look good.

The Draw tab

When you select the Draw tab the pen tool will be selected by default. From here you'll need to select what kind of pen you'd like to use. There are a number of pens, pencils and highlighters to choose from. Selecting the drop-down menu from each one enables you to select the colour, effects and thickness of each pen. There's also a helpful eraser tool for when you make a mistake... which you will.

Draw with a trackpad

Drawing with a mouse is really hard. Drawing with a trackpad is only slightly easier. If you select this option from the Draw tab you'll see an imaginary trackpad appear onscreen. This might be handy if you want to sign your work.

Right: Using the Draw with TrackPad tool makes it easier to sign your name on your presentation with a finger.

Hot Tip

If you're unhappy with your shape but have spent forever adding text, colour and effects, there's no fun in deleting it and starting again. Just click Edit Shape to change the shape style without losing the formatting. Click the cursor where you'd like to begin drawing, hold it down and then move your mouse or trackpad. When you're done drawing, double-click, otherwise the pen tool will assume you want to carry on. If you'd like to complete a shape, double-click at the point where you started drawing.

ADVANCED POWERPOINT

HYPERLINKS & CLICKABLE SLIDES

Hyperlinks allow you to insert a clickable link from one object on a PowerPoint slide which, when clicked, will summon another slide within your presentation. They can also be used to bring up a completely different presentation from within PowerPoint or a document from other Microsoft Office programs like Word or Excel. You can use a hyperlink to bring up something from your computer (music from iTunes or Spotify, or a photo from one of your albums). You can also utilize hyperlinks to load pages from the internet, send an email right from the slide or revisit a previous slide in your presentation.

CREATING A HYPERLINK

Choose the object from which you'd like to link. It can be anything within PowerPoint: a placeholder, a shape, a word or a line of text, a video, photo, chart or table. Once you've selected it with the mouse button, hit Insert from the Ribbon and choose Hyperlink (called Link on Mac).

When you select this (or hit the Control/Command+K shortcut), you'll be presented with a pop-up dialogue box, from which you have to select the item you'd like to link to (see left).

Left: Once you have chosen to add the Hyperlink through the Insert tab you must choose the item to link it to in the pop-up dialogue box.

Hyperlink to a Computer File

To bring up an existing presentation or another document on your PC/Mac, hit Insert > Link and you'll see Web Page or File as the first option. His Select Here you can select To bring up the dialogue box. Browse to the file of your choice from your computer. It may be in My Documents or maybe the Recents tab.

Hyperlink to a Slide Within the Presentation

This is a fine option if you'd like to create a Contents slide for your presentation or if you'd like to jump from one section to another within a long presentation.

From the Insert Hyperlink window select the 'Place in This Document' tab which brings up a list of all of the slides within your presentation. Clicking a slide will bring up a preview and if this is the one you'd like to link to then press OK.

Hyperlink to a Web Page

If you'd like to call on information from a page on the internet – offering further reading for your audience, a link to a video or a photo gallery – you can launch a web page from your PowerPoint presentation.

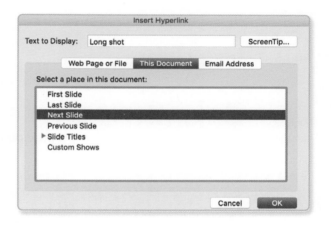

Above: You can use Hyperlinks within your presentation to jump between pages non-chronologically, for example if using a contents page.

Hot Tip

To create a Contents slide, add a new Title and Placeholder slide immediately following your first title slide. Use the content placeholder to write a numbered list of sections or slide titles and then use the Hyperlink tool to add the link to each section.

Insert Hyperlink

Text to Display: Long shot   ScreenTip...

Web Page or File   This Document   Email Address

Link to an existing file or web page.

Address: |-solutions/filmmaking-101-camera-shot-types| Select...

Cancel   OK

Above: You can add a Hyperlink to a webpage by pasting the URL into the Address box of the Insert Hyperlink pop-up window.

Hot Tip

You can only click Hyperlinks while working within the Slide Show view, so you may like to preview the presentation to test all of your links work. Only text changes its appearance when you add hyperlinks (adding a blue underline), while all other objects remain the same.

Select your object as normal and bring up the Insert link/Link Window by selecting Insert > Hyperlink (Insert > Link on a Mac). Using the web page or tab you can simply paste the relevant internet link (e.g. www.office.com) into the Address box and click OK.

Hyperlinking to an Email Address

Linking to an email address is a great idea if you want to add a little ownership of your presentation. If you type your own email address, it makes sense to provide a link to it also. When this link is clicked, it will open a blank email address in the user's email client (Outlook for PC, Mail for Mac). This is great if people in your audience are navigating through the presentation by themselves and you want to encourage further contact or feedback.

USING ACTION BUTTONS

You may recall that when we covered adding shapes to your presentation (*see* page 183) we introduced items called Action Buttons. These shapes such as, forward, back, beginning, end, home, information and more, are perfect for anchoring information within your PowerPoint presentation. They can be used to move forwards and backwards within the presentation, play a media clip or jump to the end of the presentation. They, like hyperlinked objects, can be used to launch web pages or new documents. As with Hyperlinks, Action Buttons only work when you're delivering the presentation .

Types of Action Buttons

Once you've added an Action Button, there's not always a lot of customizing you need to do, as most come loaded with actions befitting the icon. There are 12 Action Buttons to choose from and you can, of course, customize them how you wish, should you like to add a different action.

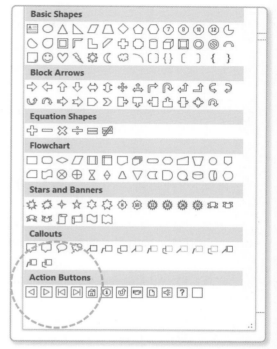

Above: Action buttons are an attractive way of controlling your slideshow. They carry commands so you can use them as links to other pages, etc, throughout your presentation.

Back: By default, adding this arrow will allow you to move back one slide.

Forward: The default action takes you forward one slide.

End: Clicking this button will take you to the end of the presentation.

Start: Return to the beginning of a presentation.

Home: Another button to take you back to the beginning.

Information: No default action, so you'll need to apply one (see below). This would be ideal for linking to an external source, such as a website or datasheet containing more info.

⊖ **Return**: The default action takes you to the last viewed slide.

⊖ **Movie**: No default action applied, but would be useful for linking to a video on your computer or on the internet.

⊖ **Document**: No default action for this button, but logic suggests you'd want to use this to launch a Word document.

⊖ **Sound**: Want to play a piece of music from within your presentation, on your computer or from the internet? Hyperlink it to this button.

⊖ **Help**: No default action for the button, but if your presentation was running in an exhibit, a help button could be used to direct visitors to further information on the internet.

⊖ **Blank**: No default action here either. Do with this as you may, or even draw your own action.

Adding Action Buttons to Your Slides

1. In order to add one of these buttons, identify the slide and click the Insert tab in the Ribbon. From the drop-down Shapes menu, you'll see Action Buttons; click on the icon that best suits your intended action.

2. Draw it on your slide as you normally would draw a shape by holding down the mouse button and dragging it to the size you want.

3. This will automatically summon the Action Settings Window, but you can also

Hot Tip
Actions can be added to any object within PowerPoint, not just the custom Action Buttons within Shapes. To add an action to a picture, text box or chart, select it and hit Insert > Action and then follow the instructions below.

bring this up by selecting Action from the Insert tab (right click the button and select Action Settings on Mac). If you're happy with the default action, just press OK, but here's where you can customize Action Buttons to your own ends.

4.   Action Buttons can be called into service by clicking on them or simply by hovering the mouse over them. You'll see the two options represented by separate tabs in the Action Settings Window. Here you can move between the two tabs (Mouse Click and Mouse Over) and then select your Action (see right).

Types of Action

Action Buttons work much like Hyperlinks. You can use the Action Settings menu to link to anywhere in your presentation, another PowerPoint presentation, another file on your computer or an internet URL. However, there are a few more options here: you can run a program like Office, Excel or iTunes, or run a Macro (a custom-built mini-program – a bit advanced for our needs, but for further reading go to Office.com/help and type in Macros). Last but not least, you can also use them to play a sound, as we did with slide transitions (see page 117).

Above: Select the action that you want your button to have by clicking on it.

Hot Tip

As with Hyperlinks, you can use the Master Slide editor to add multiple Action Buttons which appear on all of your slides.

COLLABORATING ON PRESENTATIONS

Quite often, when producing PowerPoint presentations, the responsibility for creating and delivering the slide show won't always fall on your own shoulders; work colleagues, family members or classmates are also involved. Thankfully, the software comes equipped with tools for group sharing, modification and commenting.

SHARING YOUR PRESENTATION

If you're working as a team and have taken control of the presentation, it's likely that the rest of the group are going to want to have an input on the content – and besides, it's good to have feedback from your peers. PowerPoint has plenty of sharing tools that can get your work to colleagues, quickly and easily. We explored some of these tools when saving presentations to OneDrive.

Firstly, we need to save your presentation to the cloud. Select File > Save as and select OneDrive as the location. Here you can navigate to an existing folder or select another one to store your presentation. This is what makes the presentation available to others.

Note: The following tools require a subscription version of Microsoft Office 365 to work correctly. Both yourself and the recipients of your presentation must be signed up for Office 365.

Inviting others to edit

Once the presentation is saved online, you can easily share it with friends or colleagues via the email invitation tool. This sends fellow users a link where they can access the PowerPoint presentation directly.

Select File > Share or select the omnipresent Share button in the top right corner of the app (on Office 365) and you'll be presented with several options.

Above: The Backstage View helps you to manage things like file size, permissions and performance options, so ensure you make the relevant checks before sharing your presentation.

→ **Invite People:** Here you'll need to type in email address(es) for those you wish to share with. You can also add a custom message. If you add 'Can Edit' to the tick box, those recipients will be able to make changes to the presentation. If not, they will only have read-only access. However, they will be able to add comments.

→ **Copy Link:** Here you will be able to copy a link to the presentation you can share via means other than email (direct message, etc.). Here you'll also be able to select whether the shared presentation can be edited, or just read by the recipient.

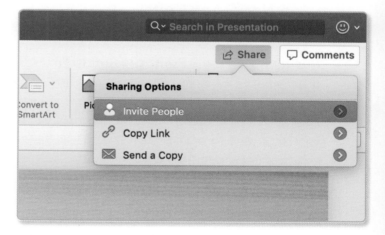

Above: Once the presentation is uploaded to OneDrive, you have a whole host of sharing options available to you.

Send As Attachment/Send Presentation (on Mac): Here you will be able to copy a link to the presentation you can share via means other than email (direct message, etc.). Here you'll also be able to select whether the shared presentation can be edited, or just read by the recipient. Selecting this option enables you to send the entire presentation as an email attachment rather than a link. This is ideal if you want to send the slides to someone for review. Selecting this option will launch your default email client with the presentation attached to a compose window. Here you can add email addresses, a subject line and a message to recipients.

Send As PDF: As above, but a PDF file is much more compressed than a presentation and will allow you to send the presentation as a manageable file size. It's also handy if you're not seeking edits, just feedback on your presentation.

Above: The File > Share tab on PC offers all manner of sharing options, the ability to copy the line, save online, send as attachment and more.

Receiving a PowerPoint presentation

If you've sent a link to your PowerPoint presentation, a person who receives that email will be invited to view it in OneDrive. Selecting this will open the free, browser-based version of PowerPoint Online. They will have the opportunity to view the document, to Edit it in the browser (if you have permitted edits), download the presentation to open on a desktop version of PowerPoint. They can also view the slideshow or print it as a PDF.

Recipients of the presentation don't need a OneDrive account or an Office 365 subscription (through Hotmail, Live.com, Outlook.com) or PowerPoint installed to view and edit the shared presentation, it will simply open in the web browser (Internet Explorer, Firefox, Chrome, etc.). It's possible to Edit within the browser.

Co-Authoring A Presentation

If you send your presentation to a fellow PowerPoint user and allow them to make edits, those edits will be synced back to your document quite quickly. You'll be able to see which person made the changes by a visual colour indicator identifying the user, if they are signed into their Microsoft account. Otherwise it will just say Guest. This is a great way to work on projects in real time, together.

Above: When a co-author makes a change, you will see that reflected when it is synced back to the presentation you're working on.

Working with Comments

Perhaps a more effective method of allowing colleagues to steam in and make wholesale changes to your presentation is to invite comments that might improve it. You'll still need to enable the editing mode (rather than read only) to apply comments. Comments made on a presentation can be replied to, deleted or marked as resolved by the author (i.e. you). You can make comments for others to address and they can make them for you.

Before You Share

Before we start distributing our presentation to the world, there are a few housekeeping matters to take care of.

Hot Tip

If you can see a colleague is working on a presentation, their avatar will show up in the Ribbon. Click this to chat with them one-on-one rather than using the comments.

Above: Collaborating on a presentation makes it possible for colleagues to make suggestions via the comments section.

Media Size and Performance (PC only): If your presentation contains lots of video or audio content, then the file could be reaching a size where sharing is difficult and, in the case of email, impossible. On PC select File > Info > and Multimedia. Here you can change video quality from between 1080p to 720p to 480p. This may take a little while to achieve as the program compresses the files.

To compress pictures: Select the option named as such from the Picture Format tab when working with images. Here you'll see a drop-down picture quality menu that offers a wide range of options. While Mac owners can't compress video, they can compress pictures.

Permissions: If you don't want others to change the presentation you can select 'Mark as Final' via File > Info > Permissions (PC only) to prevent edits or you can take the extra step of applying a password to ensure only those with the password can open the file. Mac users can apply a password by selecting File > Passwords.

Hot Tip

We ran the spell checker in Chapter 3 (*see* page **94**), but it's always wise to give it another run through.

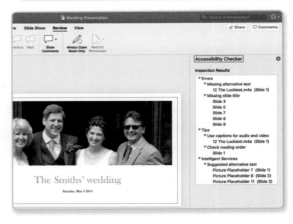

Above: The Accessibility tab will point out if it thinks your presentation will be readable by those with disability.

Accessibility: This option, available in the Review tab on PC and Mac is a good exercise to go through before sharing your presentation. It will ensure the presentation is readable by those with disabilities and it will point out any errors.

Hot Tip
If you're planning to work on an older version of PowerPoint – perhaps on old work or school PC – you should save the presentation as PowerPoint 97–2003 Presentation within the File Format portion of the Save dialogue box.

Above: Most of the Share settings for Macs are located within the top File menu.

SAVING YOUR PRESENTATION ONLINE

The PowerPoint Online app

The PowerPoint web app is a scaled back version of the desktop app. It allows users to amend text and pictures themes, and to insert pictures, SmartArt, Clip Art and links. All changes will be automatically saved back to the document on OneDrive. Everyone with whom you've shared the document will see the same version. Once everyone is happy with the changes, you can select the 'Open in PowerPoint'

Above: Recipients of the presentation can edit the document by using the Office web apps.

button and then Compare the presentation (PC only) in order to accept or reject the changes made by the group.

Above: Here is how a received PowerPoint presentation looks when you open it in a web browser like Google Chrome

Share to a SharePoint Location

This business-centric tool from Microsoft is very similar to OneDrive in that it allows users to read, edit or copy the file in real time for a master version.

SharePoint is usually a tool used by businesses to improve employee productivity and to allow them to collaborate and work together even when out of the office. If your place of work, school or college uses SharePoint, you can select this tool from the Backstage View to save the file to a shared location (File > Save As > Add A Place > Save to SharePoint). Here you'll be asked to provide a link to the shared folder on Sharepoint. If you're interested in acquiring SharePoint for your business, then head to sharepoint.microsoft.com for more information.

COMMENTING & COMPARING

Co-authoring the document isn't for everyone. The comparing tools are better for those who want to retain ownership of their presentation but would like some feedback, suggestions or corrections. As we mentioned in the sharing section, if someone in your work group has added changes through a different version of the document, or made comments, using this method they won't be synced with your document in real time, but you'll have the opportunity to review and accept/reject them by comparing two versions.

USING THE COMPARISON TOOLS (PC ONLY)

If other people in your group have made changes to the presentation, it's easy to check these against the original:

1. Save a hard copy of your presentation to your computer rather than to OneDrive. Close it.

2. Save a copy of the same presentation to OneDrive and share with whomever you wish via the Share tools mentioned in this chapter.

3. When everyone has finished reviewing the presentation and the changes are in place, re-open the original version of the presentation that you saved on your computer.

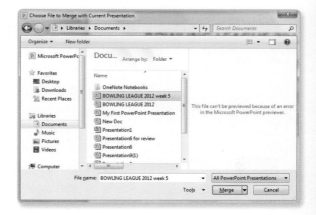

Above: By selecting Compare in the Review tab you will be requested to Merge the new and edited document.

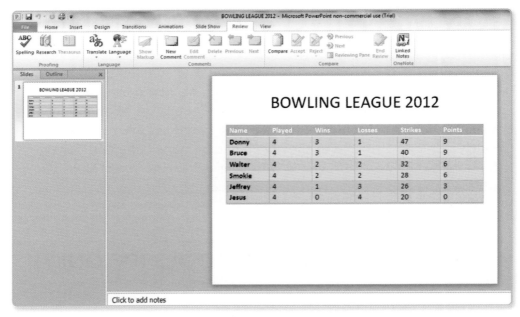

Above: PowerPoint will provide you with an action pane containing all the amendments made to each particular slide.

4. Click Review from the Ribbon and then select Compare. There's a menu to Choose File to Merge with Current Presentation. Click this to find the version that you saved to the OneDrive folder. Click Merge.

5. If people left Comments you'll see them under Slide Changes in the Revisions pane. You can address these comments by clicking on them individually. Dive deeper by clicking the Comments button in the status bar.

Left: Once you have compared changes, you can choose to accept or reject them.

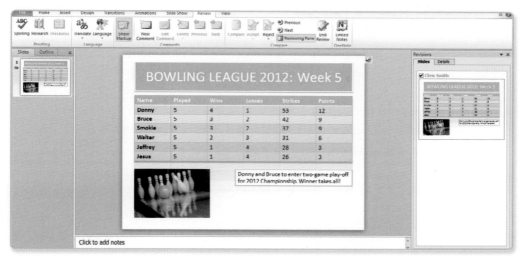

Above: No changes are made to your document until you accept them. Once you have, they will appear in the normal PowerPoint window.

6.   Changes to the presentation will be seen under Presentation Changes in the Revisions pane on the right side of the screen. Clicking an item will show details.

7.   To accept the change select the tick box next to the other actors icon. To reject it, just ignore. Nothing will be added to the presentation.

Hot Tip

No changes will be made to your document until you accept them, which means viewing them and making a judgement. To view the amended version of the slide and Accept or Reject the changes based on that, double-click the slide within the Revisions tab.

USING COMMENTS

Adding Post-it Notes-like comments to slides within PowerPoint can provide great reminders for changes you need to make or, if someone is reviewing the presentation, it can be a great way for them to make suggestions without messing with your beautifully designed slides.

Adding Comments to Slides

1. In order to add a comment, simply select the item within a slide that you'd like to comment on and hit the New Comment button (New on Mac) on the Review tab.

2. This will bring up the sticky note where you can begin to type and add your suggestions (e.g. 'I think we need a different picture here' or 'You've spelt contemporary incorrectly'.)

3. All comments will be identified within the presentation by a small indicator with the initials of the person who wrote them and the comment number (for example, CS1). Clicking this will bring up the comment note.

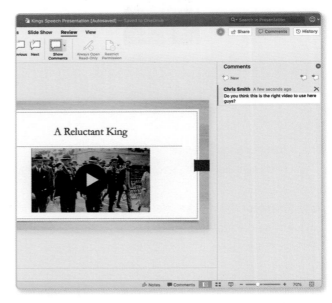

Above: You can add comments to your document for others to see when addressing editing issues.

4. You can edit the comments, delete them or move between them using the previous and next buttons on the Review tab. You can show or hide comments using the Show Markup button (Show on Mac).

TRANSPORTING YOUR PRESENTATION

If you're planning to deliver the presentation from your own computer then you won't need this section. However, if you're on the move and need to transport your entire presentation elsewhere you could always email it to yourself and share it to OneDrive or SharePoint. There are other options, though, if you want a plan B or don't have access to the internet at your new destination.

BURN TO A CD OR DVD

This is a great option for transporting your presentation if it's too large to email or upload to OneDrive/ SharePoint. In the Backstage View (File tab in the Ribbon on PC) hit Save and then select Computer. Here you can use your regular tools disk burning software to burn the presentation to a CD.

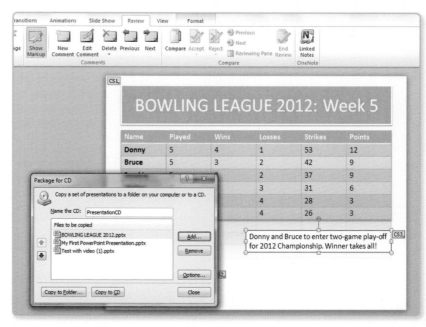

Above: A good way of transporting your presentation is by burning it onto a CD or DVD.

EXTERNAL HARD DRIVE
OR MEMORY STICK

The tech world is moving beyond CDs and DVDs as storage media; they're too easily damaged and often don't offer enough space for our needs. You may like to save your presentation to a memory stick (often called pen drives or flash drives, *see* image across the page) or a fully-fledged external hard drive. Both of these will usually plug into the USB ports of your computer.

In order to move the file to the new drive, first plug it into your computer and then open the file viewer. Now find the PowerPoint presentation(s) you'd like to take with you, copy it and then paste it within the hard drive's window (you can also just drag and drop it). Alternately, you can just save a copy of the version to the drive.

BROADCASTING AND VIDEOING

You don't have to be standing in front of your audience in order to deliver your PowerPoint presentation – in most cases you'd probably rather not be.

LET THE WHOLE WORLD SEE!

PowerPoint for PC has a feature enabling users to broadcast their presentation live to the entire world or record a video of it which can then be uploaded to the internet to be viewed any time. It can come complete with a narrated audio track recorded by you and pre-set timings for slide progression. It's much easier than you think it would be but, before we start, there are a few things we need to do to prepare our presentation. Unfortunately this is no longer available on the Mac, but you can save the presentation as a video.

CREATING A NARRATION TRACK

Before you broadcast to millions or create a video to upload on YouTube, you may want to record an audio track, as you're not going to be present to talk through the information on each of your slides:

Above: You can add narration and other audio to go alongside your slides.

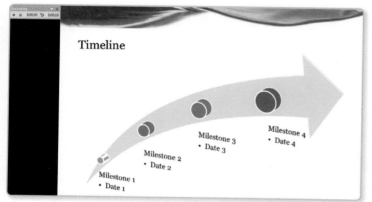

Above: Use your computer's built in microphone to record your narration, and keep track of the time by looking at the Recording box in the top left-hand corner.

1. From the Slide Show menu select Record Slide Show. This will take you into the Presenter View, which shows the number of slides, the current slide, the next slide and timers. The timer will commence when you hit record.

2. Speak into the built-in microphone on your computer and your narrations will be recorded. When you've progressed through the slide show and it comes to an end, the presentation will be recorded along with the narrations.

3. To ensure that they play during a broadcast or video recording, make sure the Play Narrations box is ticked within the Set Up pane of the Slide Show tab.

Timings

If you'd rather control the presentation by hand during the broadcast, you can deselect Use Timings. For a video you'll need timings, as you'll be unable to control it yourself. Therefore, when creating the video PowerPoint will ask you to choose how long you want it to dwell on each slide (this is set at 5 seconds).

Hot Tip

The internal microphone on most computers isn't great. If you would like your audience to decipher your words our advice would be to invest in a USB microphone. They're usually plug-and-play, which means you can insert them into your USB port and they'll take over as the default mic on your computer.

RECORD WITH THE LASER POINTER (PC ONLY)

As you're not going to be physically present to point to the most important information, you can use PowerPoint's built-in laser pointer functionality when recording a slide show.

Above: If you decide to make your presentation into a video, you need to choose how many seconds you want to spend on each slide.

To add a laser pointer to your broadcast or video, click Record Slide Show and make sure that the Narrations and laser pointer box is ticked, and then start to record. To bring up the laser pointer, press and hold down Control and the left mouse button on your PC, and then move the mouse or trackpad around. To move to the next slide, release Ctrl, and then click the left mouse button. When you have finished recording the slide show, the laser will be included in the broadcast or video.

Hot Tip

When recording your slide show to broadcast or for video, don't talk while moving between slides. Finish your sentence and pause. This will prevent you being cut off in mid-sentence when you progress through the presentation.

BROADCASTING YOUR PRESENTATION

OK – now we're ready to go live! This is one of the cleverest tricks in the book (both this book and PowerPoint's!). Your presentation can be broadcast live to anyone with an internet connection and a computer; they don't even need PowerPoint, as it's totally web-browser based. All that's needed is for you to log into your Microsoft-based email account (Windows Live, Hotmail, etc.) to start the broadcast. Just like a conference call, a link will simply be sent to recipients who you want to tune in.

Starting a Web Broadcast (PC Only)

No set-up is required to broadcast the presentation. A link is created to share with people and anyone with the link can see it. If you choose it can be available for viewers to download. Here's what you need to do in order to begin broadcasting a presentation:

Above: You can choose to start a broadcast from the Share option in the Backstage View on PC.

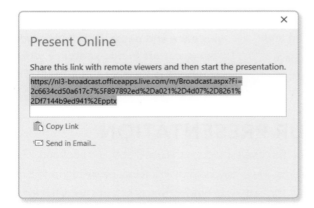

Above: Once PowerPoint has connected to the Broadcast Service you will be given a web link to send to your recipients.

1. Select File (the Backstage View) > Share > Broadcast Slide Show. This launches the Office Presentation Service window.

2. Choose whether you want remote viewers to download the presentation and hit Present Online.

3. Here you'll be asked to sign in to your Microsoft account if you haven't already.

4. Microsoft will generate the link for you to share with attendees. You can copy and paste it or share in an email. Recipients will be able to click on the link to join the broadcast.

5. The presentation won't commence until you click Start Presentation.

6. To end your online presentation, press Escape to get out of the Slide Show View and then select End Online Presentation in the Present Online tab. You'll be asked to confirm.

Delivering the Broadcast

If you've added timings, narrations and a laser-pointer guide to your presentation then you don't have to do anything once you've hit Start Slide Show. The presentation will run simultaneously on your screen and that of the viewers.

When the presentation is complete, the broadcast will end. If you're going to control the slides by hand, you can use all of the tools normally available to you (*see* page 81). As you click Next Slide, Previous Slide, Play a media item, and so on, the change will be reflected on your viewers' screens within fractions of a second. All animations, transitions and effects will also be visible to your audience. Pretty cool, huh?

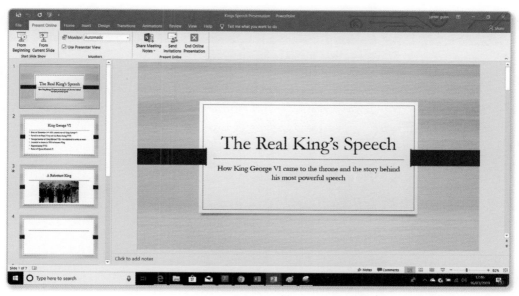

Above: As you control the presentation, your recipients will experience what is happening on your screen.

MAKE A VIDEO

The second way to ensure your presentation reaches your audience without you being physically in the room is by creating a video of your presentation. This video can be shared on DVD, memory stick, or it can be placed on an online storage portal (like OneDrive) or uploaded to a video sharing site like YouTube.

A video version of the presentation is also a great backup to have if you know you'll be presenting somewhere without PowerPoint or the internet. There are few nuances between the PC and Mac versions of PowerPoint; here's how to create a video for both.

How to Create a Video on a Mac

Because you can't broadcast your presentation from the Mac, the video tool is especially important. Once you've completed your presentation, added the laser pointer and recorded the timings and narration you're ready to save it as a video. It's easy.

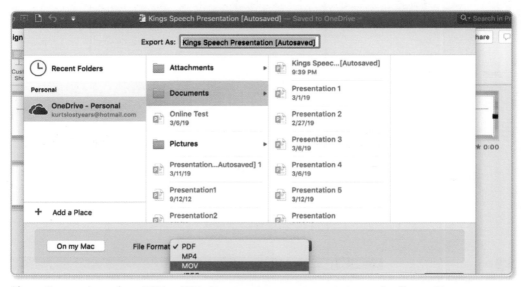

Above: You can choose from .MOV or .MP4 when exporting your presentation to a video file on a Mac.

1.   Select File > Export.

2.   Select a File Format from the
      drop down menu. You can
      choose an .MOV or and MP4
      file. Choose the latter for the
      greatest compatibility with
      all formats.

> **Hot Tip**
>
> **If you're watching the video on a
> Mac, download the VLC video player,
> which will embrace the Microsoft format
> on your Apple machine.**

3.   Next you'll be able to add the presentation quality and choose whether you want to use the
      timings. If not you can set how many seconds you wish to spend on each slide by default.

4.   After that, choose a location and a name for the file and hit Export. It will save to your
      computer or the online location or your choosing.

5.   Beware, this might take a while, but once complete, you can do as you wish.

How to Create a Video on PC

The method here is slightly different. From File > Export hit Create a Video. Again you'll need
to select quality and whether to use the narrations and timings. Next, click Create Video and
choose the folder and file name. Finally, click Save. Depending on the file size, it'll take a few
minutes to export the video.

> **Hot Tip**
>
> **If you plan to export your presentation as a video from the get-go, you might prefer
> to design the slides in the widescreen (16:9) aspect ration (see page 49). This will
> ensure that the slide show fills the screen without any unsightly black borders.**

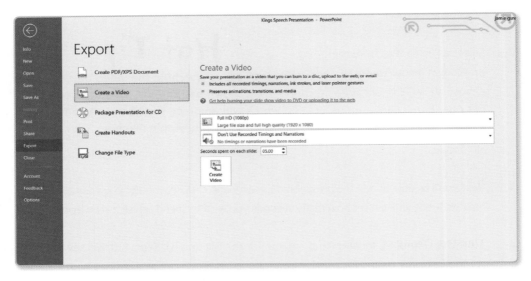

Above: On a PC, create a video from the Export pane within the Backstage View tab.

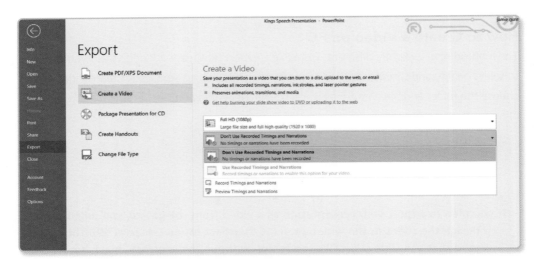

Above: Within the Create a Video options you can alter the default settings concerning timings and narration.

Uploading Your Video to the Internet

The final step in the video creation process is the most important. In order to deliver it to the masses, so they can access your beautiful slide show on-demand, you'll need to upload it to the internet. We'd suggest the most popular solution on the planet: YouTube. Uploading is criminally simple, but here are the key steps.

1.   Go to www.youtube.com and log in (you'll need a free Google account or Gmail address).

2.   Hit the Upload button at the top right of the YouTube homepage and select Upload video.

3.   On the next screen, hit the Select files to upload. Choose the video from the stored location on your computer and that will start the upload. You can also select Public, Unlisted, Private or Scheduled.

4.   While the video is uploading you can type in a title, write a description and add tags. When complete hit Done.

5.   Once the upload is complete, copy the link to the video and send it to your students, work colleagues, family members or whomever you'd like.

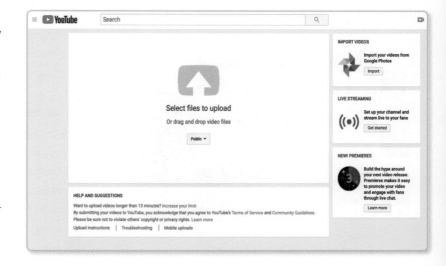

Right: Uploading your video to YouTube is simple if you stick to the steps here.

SLIDE LIBRARIES

PowerPoint contains plenty of tools to cut down on the amount of work you have to do. Slide Masters (see page 128) allow you add common objects to all slides, while you can easily duplicate slides when minimal changes are required. Another way, which we've not yet covered, is to pull them in from other presentations. This is perfect if you've created a host of stunningly designed presentation slides that you'd like to use over and over again for new presentations, or those where few changes are required.

IMPORTING SLIDES

1. When selecting a New Slide from the home tab, hit Reuse Slides from the very bottom of the drop-down menu. This will launch the pane you'll see to the right of the screen below (it's all done from a pop-up window on Mac).

Above: You can insert slides by using the Reuse Slides button from the New Slide drop-down menu.

2. Click the Insert Slide From option on PC (it's already selected on Mac), choose the presentation from which you'd like to borrow a slide and then click Open.

3. This will display the thumbnail images of slides from that presentation within the Reuse pane (pop-up window on Mac). Click them to automatically insert the slide within your current presentation. You can also choose to keep the source formatting, otherwise they'll confirm to your presentation.

4. All features of the imported slide will remain the same.

Using Slide Libraries

This is an option that will not be available to the vast majority of PowerPoint users as it requires your school or office to be signed up with Microsoft SharePoint (see page 203) and requires Microsoft PowerPoint Professional Plus (there's no way we're forking out for that!) but it's a really handy tool nonetheless.

SharePoint allows multiple users access to a library of PowerPoint slides created by multiple people. It's perfect if your team creates a lot of PowerPoint presentations where uniform information and design are required. If you know this functionality is already set up in your office you can easily publish slides to SharePoint or, in turn, grab from the library to use in your own presentations.

↪ **To publish slides to SharePoint (PC only):** Hit File to enter Backstage View, select Share and then click Publish Slides. Then select the slides you'd like to publish, enter the URL for the library (you'll need to grab this from your system administrator, i.e. call the IT guy!) and hit Publish.

↪ **To import a slide from SharePoint (PC only):** From the Reuse Slides pane (see screenshot on page 216) hit the Browse button and select Open Slide Library; this will give you options from the shared library. Then to select the presentation use the same methods explained in the Reuse Slides section on page 216.

Macros

Macros are mini programs written by users to help perform regular, yet time-consuming, tasks within Microsoft Office programs such as PowerPoint (this feature lives within the View tab). The idea is that a number of actions that usually take several steps can instead be performed in one keyboard short cut. There's little reason for us to investigate them at the moment, but if you'd like to learn more head to www.office.com and search for Macros in the support pages.

POWERPOINT PROJECTS

PROJECT 1: RE-CREATING HISTORY FOR TEACHERS AND STUDENTS

PowerPoint can be a great classroom tool and here we'll show you how to create a simple history-based presentation. Bulleted lists can point out the key facts and SmartArt can relay a sequence of events, while audio and YouTube clips furnish the presentation with entertaining, interesting content from further sources. Here's a step-by-step guide to creating a slide show we'll call 'The Real King's Speech'.

1. Open PowerPoint. Begin a Blank Presentation from the gallery. Hit the Design tab in the Ribbon to select a theme from the drop-down menu. This particularly regal presentation would be best served by the Organic theme, which should now adorn the first slide.

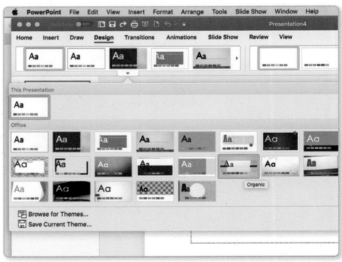

Step 1: Choose a design that will reflect the theme of your presentation (PowerPoint for Mac shown).

2. Choose a title and subtitle (try to keep both within two lines to ensure they are neat and highly visible). Click within the pre-set boxes and start to type.

3. Click Control+M (Control+Shift+N on Mac) to add a new slide (repeat this step whenever adding a new slide). By default, this will add a Title and Content placeholder slide. Give the slide a title and then click within the content placeholder. After every piece of text information, hit the Enter key to create a new bullet point.

4. Add a video from YouTube to break up the text-based slides. Using a new slide, hit Layout from the Home tab and select the Title Only option. Select the Insert tab, click the video icon and select Video from Web Site.

Step 2: Try to fit your text within the pre-set boxes.

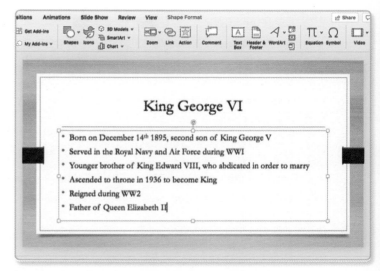

Step 3: Pressing Enter after each point will create a bulleted list.

Enter the URL for the online video:

Your use of online videos is subject to each provider's Terms of Use and Privacy Policy.

Learn more   Cancel   Insert

Step 5: The URL will link your slide to the video of your choice.

5. Head to www.youtube.com and find your clip. Copy the embed code (*see* page 150 for instructions) and paste that into the Insert Video from > Online Movie dialogue box open on your slide.

6. Press OK. Resize the video by dragging on the corners and position it where you need it on the slide by picking up the object with your cursor and moving it into place.

7. On a new slide, select the Comparison layout. Click on the relevant placeholder, select the Insert Image icon, choose the pictures from the folder where they are saved on your computer and click Insert. In this

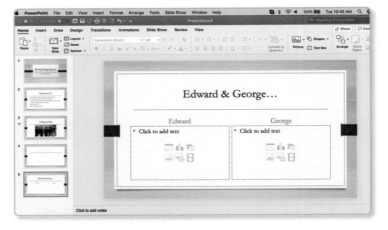

Step 7: Encourage feedback from the class by asking for comparisons between the brothers.

case, feature pictures of Edward VII and George VI, and call upon the class to discuss the difference between the two men.

8. Adding further text-based slides at this point would be acceptable without risking information overload but be careful of running too many text-only slides in a row. Add the new Title and Content slide, and add the information as you did in Step 3.

As this particular slide represents a timeline of information, we can convert text to a SmartArt diagram. Once you've highlighted the bulleted list (Control+A selects all text), right-click, hit Convert to SmartArt and select the Staggered Process diagram from the Process category within the SmartArt Graphics menu in the SmartArt Design tabs.

9. Select the SmartArt diagram and then click the Animations tab. Choose the Float In animation and then choose One by One from the Group Graphic section of the SmartArt Animations tab of the Effect Options drop-down menu. This will ensure the points arrive on screen at your command.

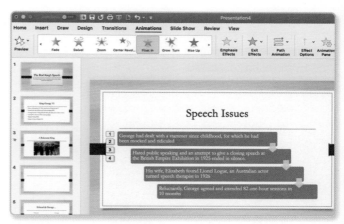

Step 9: The points seen here will arrive one by one if you choose Float In from the Animations tab.

10. In order to add an end-of-slide show quiz for the class, use one bullet for each question and a secondary paragraph for the answer. To add a secondary paragraph, press the Tab key on the keyboard to indent it underneath the previous point. Then follow the instructions listed in Step 9 to ensure the question and then the answers appear in stages using Animations.

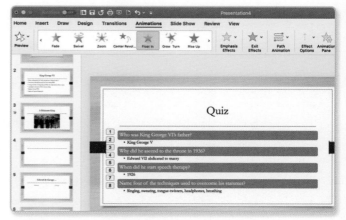

Step 10: To retain the audience's attention, have the answers to your end-of-show quiz float in via the Animations tab.

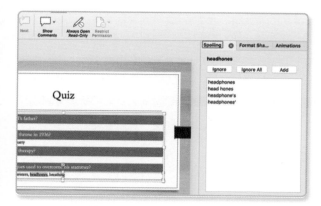

Step 11: Use the Spell Check to ensure your presentation does not look slap-dash and amateur.

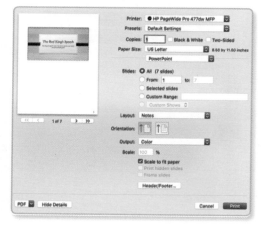

Step 13: Remember to print out your prompt notes, and also handouts for your classmates.

11. Select the Spelling tool from within the Review tab. You can accept or ignore suggested corrections and add words to the dictionary. Once the check is done, you'll see a message that says: 'The spelling check is complete'.

12. Revisit the slides and add Transitions. Select the slide you want to move to (not from) and click the Transitions tab from the Ribbon. Click on the transition of your choice (e.g. Split, Push, Wipe) and you'll see an instant preview on screen. Use the Timing pane to control how long a transition lasts and whether a sound is played. Hit the Apply To All button to add your transitions to every slide.

13. Add notes to help deliver the presentation and ensure all talking points are covered. Enter the Notes tab at the bottom of each slide and type the information you'd like to recall. To print Notes Pages click Control+P/Command+P and then select Notes Pages from the Print Layout menu (from this menu, you can also print handouts).

14. Connect to the external monitor (*see* page 73) and select the Slide Show tab. From that tab select Presenter View (*see* page 83) and begin your presentation. Move between slides or bullet points with the up/down arrows (for a full list of in-presentation tools *see* pages 81–82). When the show is over, click the Escape key.

PROJECT 2: TEACHING A FILM-MAKING CLASS

Traditionally, in order to teach a film class, a teacher would need a whiteboard (or blackboard), printed handouts and a DVD player – at least. This case study is an example of how PowerPoint can encapsulate multiple classroom tools to produce an interactive, all-in-one solution. Designed using PowerPoint PC, this is a slide show about basic film-making vocabulary and is illustrated by text, photos and videos.

1. Open PowerPoint. From the PowerPoint Presentation Gallery, select Main Event from the options.

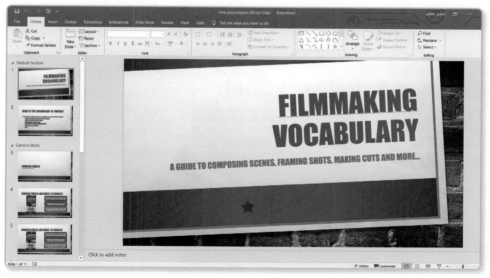

Step 1: The Main Event Theme looks extremely effective for this subject matter.

2. Add a title and subtitle to the Title slide. Next, add a New Slide, by clicking that button within the Home tab. Create a text-based slide that embellishes upon your title by adding bullet points that summarise the topics to be covered during the class.

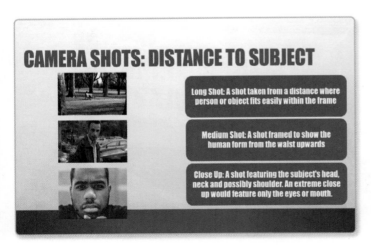

WHAT IS THE VOCABULARY OF CINEMA?

- THE GLOSSARY OF COMMON TERMS USED BY FILMMAKERS TO DESCRIBE FILMING TECHNIQUES:
  - CAMERA SHOTS (ESTABLISHING, CLOSE-UP, OVER THE SHOULDER)
  - CAMERA CUTS (JUMP, CROSS-CUT, CUT-AWAY)
  - CAMERA MOVEMENT (PAN, ZOOM, DOLLY)
  - SCENE COMPOSITION (*MISE-EN-SCENE* JUXTAPOSITION)
  - SOUND (DIEGETIC, EXTRA DIEGETIC)
  - RULES

Step 2: After the title slide, your first main slide should summarise what the presentation will cover.

3. In order to start a new section, add a New Slide and then hit Create New Section from the Home tab; this will position a section between the two slides. Type a name for the section (we've called it 'Camera Shots'). Here you could ask the class to participate by naming shots they're familiar with before delving into detail on the next slide.

CAMERA SHOTS: DISTANCE TO SUBJECT

Long Shot: A shot taken from a distance where person or object fits easily within the frame

Medium Shot: A shot framed to show the human form from the waist upwards

Close Up: A shot featuring the subject's head, neck and possibly shoulder. An extreme close up would feature only the eyes or mouth.

Steps 4 and 5: Combine SmartArt and photos to illustrate your points.

4. Add a New Slide and add text to the Title placeholder. Use the bullet points to Draw type descriptions of the close, medium and long shots. Use the Convert to SmartArt tool to create more attractive text boxes.

5. Next, add a series of images to showcase a long shot, medium shot and close-up. You can find Creative Commons images by hitting Insert > Picture > Online Pictures.

6.   Hit Command+D to create a Duplicate Slide, which will appear directly underneath. This will create a carbon copy, allowing you simply to replace the information rather than redesigning from scratch. In this slide you could add related terms, such as over-the-shoulder, crane, high angle, overhead, etc.

7.   On the next New Slide, insert a pre-prepared video clip from your computer (Insert > Video > Video On My PC) which showcases each of the shots mentioned. Ask the class to point out the long, medium and close-up shots as they happen. Select the Video Playback tab, and select Play Full Screen.

8.   Repeat Steps 3 and 4. Call the new section 'Camera Cuts'.

9.   Design the new section (and subsequent sections) in the same way. Remember you can copy and paste slides to save design time and retain consistency. Just right-click the appropriate slide and hit Copy; then right-click again underneath the last slide in the show and press Paste. For illustrating Camera Cuts, replace the thumbnail images with videos from your computer.

Step 7: Insert your video-clip and position it in the centre of the slide.

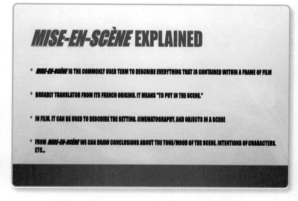

10. For the section entitled *Mise-en-scène Explained* (meaning 'what's in the frame') you could add a class exercise. Use a slide of bullet points to explain the definition of the term.

Step 10: Bulleted lists are a good way to prompt discussion.

11. Next, add a New Slide containing a video of a famous film scene from your computer (any scene from Martin Scorsese's *Taxi Driver* should work!). Use the text formatting tools to add emphasis to the keywords in the title. Show the video and then give the class five minutes to write down observations on the *mise en scène* employed by the film-maker and how it reflects upon the intended tone and meaning of the scene.

12. At the end of the video you could also add a quiz to test what the class gleaned from the presentation. Add a new section and call it 'Quiz'.

13. Add a New Slide, and apply the Title and Content. Click inside the title placeholder and type Quiz. Add the question and answer as bullet points in the Content Placeholder. Select the text and convert to SmartArt. Then, add an Entrance Effect from the Animations tab, then One by One from the Group Graphic section of the SmartArt

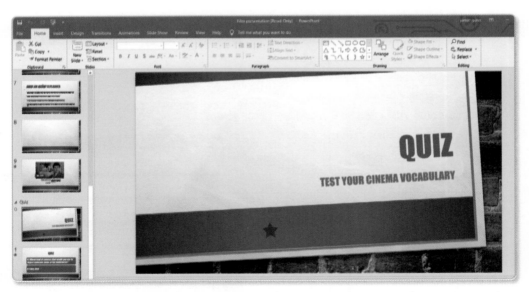

Step 13: A quiz after the video clip should guarantee your audience sits up and takes notice: after all, the purpose of a presentation is to teach them something!

Animations tab of the Effect Options drop-down menu. Repeat this step for each question.

14. Save the presentation (Control+S/Command+S on a Mac).

15. In order to save the presentation online, where it can be accessed by colleagues and absent students, select File > Save > Add Places > OneDrive. Insert Windows ID login details and select Save. If the presentation contains video it may take a while (for full details on sharing via OneDrive, *see* page 40).

16. Spellcheck your slide show for errors (Tools > Spelling).

17. Use the Notes tab on each slide to add text-based reminders of the talking points you'd like to touch upon when discussing the contents of the presentation. This way, you won't forget anything.

18. Connect your laptop or computer to the in-class projector or external monitor using a HDMI or VGA cable (depending on the newness of your equipment) and use the display's remote control to select the correct input.

19. Select the Slide Show tab and select Presenter View. This showcases the current slide, next slide, slide notes and how long the slide show has been running. It'll also display the time of day to help ensure you don't overrun. Use the keyboard and mouse tools outlined in Chapter two (*see* pages 81–82) to deliver the slide show.

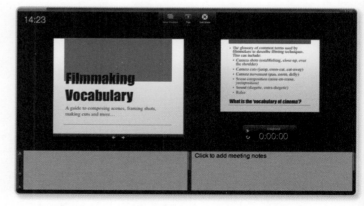

Step 19: Presenter View will give you a behind-the-scenes look at your presentation, including how much time you've taken to deliver it.

PROJECT 3:
THE FAMILY PHOTO ALBUM

PowerPoint allows excitable dads the world over to finally ditch the photo slide show carousel and create attractive photo slide shows in double-quick time for the whole family to ~~endure~~, sorry, enjoy. In this case study, we'll create an album from a template using PowerPoint 2019 for Mac with Office 365.

1. Open PowerPoint from the P icon in the Dock. This will present the PowerPoint Presentation Gallery. If an existing presentation pops up, you can select Command+Shift+P to bring up the New From Template Window.

2. There are no photo albums available within the default themes, but we can search for them to bring them up from the template archives. Just type 'wedding' into the search bar to see wide range of options. Here we'll select 'simple wedding album' and hit Create.

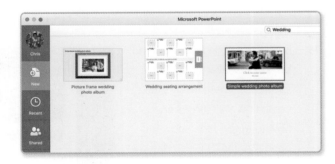

Step 2: Type 'wedding' into the search box to bring up a couple of options for creating a photo album.

3. On the Title slide, click on the photo and hit Backspace/ Delete to delete the placeholder. Then click the Insert tab in the ribbon followed by Pictures and then from File. Ideally you'll have collated all of the photos you need beforehand.

4. Find the picture you'd like to use as the cover and hit Insert. You may need to reposition it to achieve the optimum framing so hit the drop-down Crop arrow from the Picture Format page and select Fill. This will enable you to drag the photo into the optimum position. Click off the picture when done.

5. The Template features a number of pre-set slide designs. Move to the next slide and repeat the process, adding titles and subtitles to each photo you add.

6. All slides in the template are fully customisable, meaning you can select Slide Layout from the Home tab in order to see alternatives. Here we're selecting a layout with a single full-slide photo.

7. Templates feature a pre-set number of slides, and this one has a whopping 30 slides attached to it. You can adhere to that number or choose to delete slides by right-clicking on individual slides on the left side of the screen and hitting delete.

Step 4: The Fill tool in the Crop menu lets you reposition your photos within a text box.

Step 6: The slides within each template have a default layout which can be changed by going to Home tab > Layout.

Step 8: The Picture Format tab contains features and effects that will give your PowerPoint album a professional touch.

Step 10: Unlike traditional photo albums, your PowerPoint album can feature video alongside the photographs.

8. The full range of picture styles and format tools are available. You can add soft edges, frames and effects from the Picture Format tab, as you can see left. You can also choose to make photos black and white for artistic effect. To do this, select Colour from the Picture Format tab and select Grayscale.

9. If you're planning to present this to an audience, it's also possible to add a video clip for good measure. Insert a Title and Content slide, and select the Video icon from the placeholder and choose your ideo. In the Format Movie tab select Poster Frame to add an image that shows before you play the video.

10. In order to add a video, insert a Title and Content slide, and select the Video icon from the placeholder. Select the

video from your computer and it will be inserted into the slide. In the Format Movie tab select Poster Frame to add an image that shows before you play the video.

11. Because the template is pre-made you might want to rearrange the order of your slides. Hit Slide Show from the Ribbon and select Slide Sorter view. Here you can drag around the various slides until you're happy with the positions.

Step 11: Using the Slide Sorter View, it's easy to rearrange your slides before you show the album to your family.

12. A wedding album presentation is nothing without some nice smooth transitions from one slide to another. Here's where the Animations tab comes in. This presentation features a simple fade from one slide to another, but you can get fancier and add animations for each individual slide on your presentation (see page 117).

13. What's a wedding slide show without the first dance song included? Head to your title slide and hit Insert > Audio from the ribbon. Find the song of your choice in the Audio Browser or From File and select Insert. Drag the audio button to a less conspicuous place on the slide and head to the Audio Playback tab. Here you can select Play Across all Slides. If you want to get really fancy, you can select Fade In and Fade Out timings and Trim the Audio so it matches up perfectly with your presentation.

Step 13: Adding an audio file to your presentation will add a little more poignancy to proceedings.

14. Once you've added all photos and filled all the slides you wish with text, animations and more, Save your presentation (Command+S). Choose a name and location for your presentation as you do so.

15. Hook your laptop up to your HDTV using a HDMI or VGA cable. Select the corresponding Input on your TV set and deliver the presentation from the Slide Show tab (use the mouse/keyboard tools set out on pages 81–82).

16. If you're connecting with someone further afield, you can save the presentation as a video file by hitting File > Export and choosing .MP4 from the file format drop-down menu. From here, you can then share it directly, or upload it to YouTube (see page 211).

Step 16: Go to Record Slide Show to create a narration track.

17. If you're thinking of making a video you may wish to create a narration track before you broadcast. Select the Slide Show tab, hit Record Slide Show and talk about each slide (for more instructions see page 207). The track is recorded by your computer's internal microphone. Press Escape when complete and ensure Use Narrations is ticked in the Set Up pane.

PROJECT 4: THE FAMILY DIET AND FITNESS REGIME

Believe it or not, there are endless uses for PowerPoint in the home beyond the traditional family photo album. This case study will tackle the unenviable task of convincing the troops that fewer treats and more exercise is actually a good idea. It will feature the foods that have to go, make the alternatives seem exciting and outline a regime for the new, healthier era. This presentation is designed using PowerPoint 2016 for PC.

1. Open PowerPoint. This will bring up a new Blank Presentation, featuring a single Title Slide. Select the Design tab in the Ribbon and choose a theme from the drop-down menu in the centre of the pane. The Savon theme feels clean and sleek.

2. Add a title and subtitle to your slide by clicking within each of the respective placeholders and typing. This presentation is called 'Operation Work for Bacon: A Fitter, Healthier Family'.

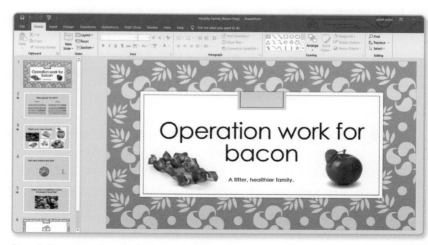

Step 2: Type your title and subtitle into the placeholders.

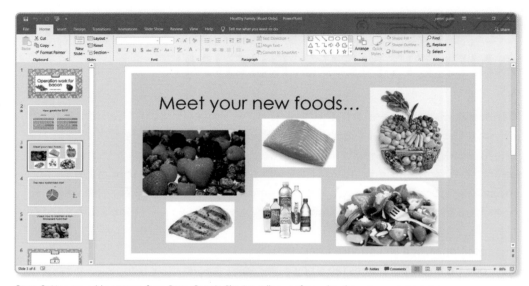

Step 3: You can add an image from PowerPoint's Clip Art gallery, or from elsewhere on your computer.

3.   Next, you can add some images to the title slide. Select Insert > Picture and then choose Online Picture. Type in what you want to add (in our case an apple and some bacon) and press Enter. From the search results click the image of your choice and it will appear on the slide. In order to resize and reposition, use the handles on the edge of the image box and then drag the whole box to where you want it. Here you might want to delete the alt text and captions boxes.

4.   Add a New Slide (Control+M) and then select Layout to the select Comparison design. You can use this to create competing bullet-pointed lists of goals. Hit convert to SmartArt from the Home tab to make them look better. Use the animation tools explained on page 118 to improve the flow of information.

5.   Add a New Slide (Control+M). Right-click it in the Slide Sorter View and select Layout. Change to Title Only. Use this slide to add pictures (*see* Step 3) of foods that will be

eliminated. If you're feeling fancy here, you can experiment with the Remove Background tool in the Picture Format menu.

6. Add an Exit Effect animation for each individual image to make them disappear from the slide (click the Image, then Animations, Exit Effects, Fade) with each click of the mouse.

7. Repeat this on the next slide, in reverse order, but use healthier food pictures from Online Picture. Once the images have been positioned, add an Entrance Effect to each one from the Animations tab. They will appear on screen with each click.

Hot Tip

For Step 5, Office 365 subscribers can let the Microsoft Design Ideas take over here. When adding multiple images to slides you should see proactive prompts from the tool in the pane, otherwise hit Design Ideas from the Design tab at any time.

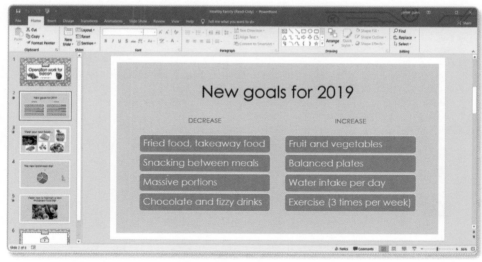

Step 7: Follow Step 4 to create competing lists of bullet points.

8. You can get a little fancier with the animation too. In order to emphasise each of the images you've added, you can add an animation as a sound effect. Group the images together by holding Shift and clicking each of them. Next, hit Animations and select Emphasis Effects and choose Teeter. Next, head to the Animation Pane on the right of the display and change the duration to 5 seconds under the Timing section. Next, select the drop-down sound menu and choose Applause.

9. In order to add a pie chart to showcase a balanced diet, create a new Title and Content slide and use the Chart icon within the placeholder to select Pie. Excel should now launch next to PowerPoint. Add your titles and percentage figures to the Excel datasheet and they'll translate to the chart automatically. You can use Add Chart Element and Chart Layout tools (*see* page 172) in the Chart Design tab to further customize your chart.

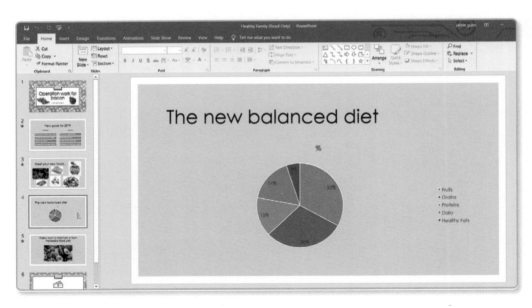

Step 9: If you want to add a chart to your presentation, Excel and PowerPoint work together to do it for you.

10. On the next slide, insert a video from YouTube to showcase alternatives to the current meals. Select Insert > Video > Online Video. Copy and paste the YouTube link to insert the clip.

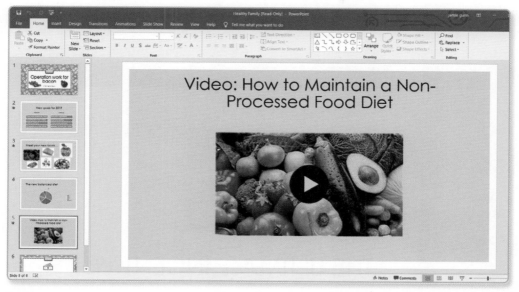

Step 10: Why not add a video for some extra inspiration? It's easy to do, and you could insert a different clip every week.

11. To illustrate the new fitness regime, add a new slide and click the Table icon from the placeholder. Select eight rows and five columns (enough for the seven days and four family members) and fill in the activities for each person to correspond with the day of the week.

12. Add a new slide with the Section Header layout to begin work on the Rewards section.

13. Create a bullet-pointed list of incentives on a new slide. Use Animations to ensure each point appears one at a time on the screen.

14. On the final slide ('The Ultimate Incentive' – *see* next page for screenshot) add a teaser link to the main reward. Highlight the 'Click here' portion of the text, hit the Insert tab, press Hyperlink (*see* page 188) and copy the URL from a website into the address box of the pop-up window (this could reveal a holiday destination like Disney World) and select OK. Remember that the link will only work in Slide Show mode.

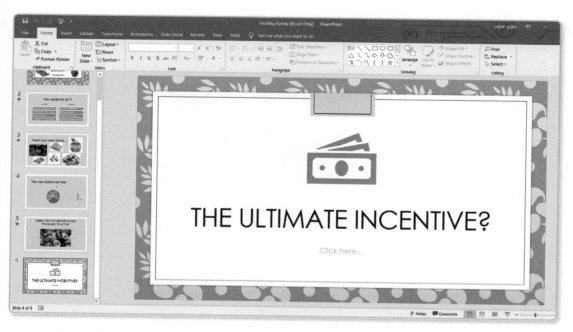

Step 14: Use what you learned in Chapter five about Hyperlinks to add one to your slideshow.

15. As you're delivering the presentation to a small family unit, have them gather round the screen. Press F5 on the keyboard to enter Presentation Mode and use the mouse/keyboard tools explained on pages 81–82 to control the presentation. Press Escape when the presentation is complete.

PROJECT 5: THE OFFICE PITCH

When you're building a case for change, PowerPoint can be one of the most powerful tools you can harness. You can use a slide show packed with charts, figures, videos and facts to convince your colleagues that your way is the right way. In this case study, we're convincing the company that Mac computers should replace PCs. This presentation is built using PowerPoint for Mac 2019 with an Office 365 subscription, which is the latest and best way to use Office.

1. Select the PowerPoint icon from the Dock on your Mac computer. Select File > New From Template. Circuit is a nice one to use here because of the tech connection.

2. Even though themes carry colour schemes, slide designs, fonts and more, you aren't limited to using those. To select a different font pairing, choose Fonts from the Theme Options pane of the Themes tab. We've chosen the Century Gothic fonts.

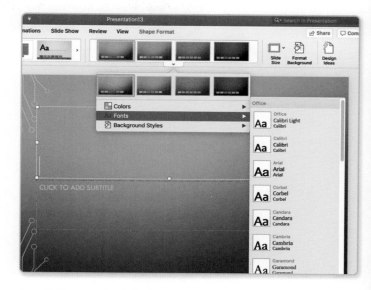

3. Click your mouse within the placeholders and begin typing text. We've called the slideshow 'PC vs Mac' with the subtitle 'Time for a change?'

Step 2: Play around with the font pairings to try out different combinations (Design tab > Theme Options > Fonts).

4. Insert photos of the 'Mac' and 'PC' computers onto the Title page using the Picture from File option within the Home tab. Here the Design Ideas tab should come into play, offering new options for your title slide. Select your favourite.

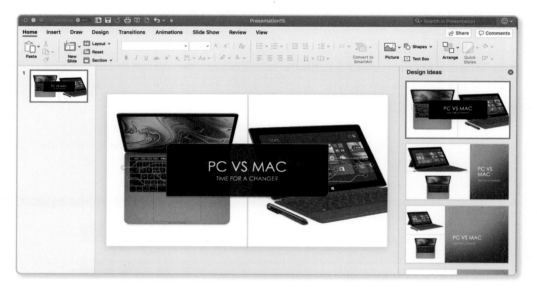

Step 4: By using the Design Ideas suggestions, PowerPoint will help you make slides look much better without you putting lots of effort into reformatting slides and images.

5. In order to make the 'Mac' image fly in and the PC image fly out, select the Mac, hit the Animations tab and click 'Fly In' from the Entrance Effects pane. In the Effect Options pane choose From Left and increase the duration to 1 second.

6. Repeat this on the 'PC' image but select Fly Out from the Exit Effects and From Right from the Effect Options men and increase the duration to 2 seconds. Select the Preview button to see how it looks.

7. Hit New Slide from the Home tab within the Ribbon. We've typed 'The Proposal' into the Title box, but the font feels too small so we've selected the text (Command+A) and used the Increase Font Size button in the Home tab to bump up the font.

8. Type in the proposal points and press Enter after each one to create a new bullet point. Hit the Animations tab, select all text (Command+A) and add Blinds from the Entrance Effects pane. This will ensure that each point arrives one at a time when presenting. Repeat this process for all additional text-based slides.

9. On a new slide, click the Video icon from the Insert Tab and select Online Video. Copy in a link from YouTube.To make the clip start automatically when the slide appears, click Start and select Automatically from the Video Playback screen. Also select Play in full screen to enhance the visibility.

Step 9: Using the tools within the Video Playback pane, you can make your video clip start automatically when you reach that particular slide.

10. On a new slide, select the Comparison Layout option from the Home tab. In each content placeholder select the Insert Chart icon and choose from the Bar Chart options. This will summon Microsoft Excel with a datasheet that will populate your chart. Replace the data in Excel with the figures and categories of your choice. Changes will be reflected in the on-screen charts. For disclosure, we made up these figures. They're not real.

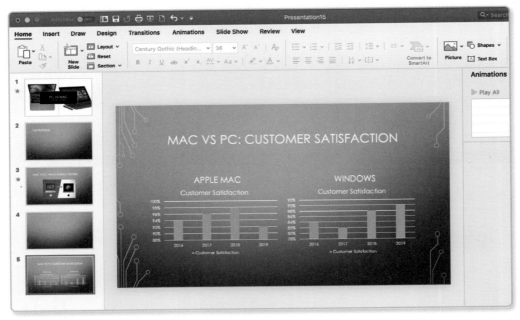

Step 10: You can add one or more charts to your slide to give a visual illustration of the points you're attempting to make.

11. Add a 'voice' from employees. Select the SmartArt tab from the Ribbon. Hit the List pane and select Vertical Picture Accent. Click on the picture placeholder and insert photos of the spokespeople. Use the Crop tools in Picture Format to ensure faces appear within the frame. You can fill the speech boxes with soundbite text by clicking within them and typing.

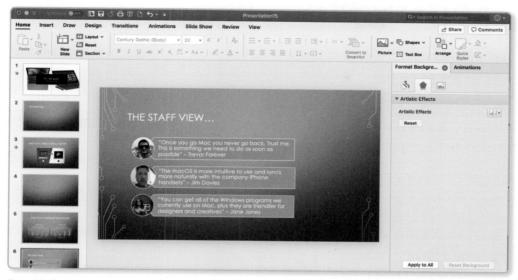

Step 11: Try the various options within SmartArt to give your presentation a professional edge.

12. Add a new Blank Side (New Slide > Layout > Blank). Draw a text box and add the title 'Questions'. Select the text and use Text Effects from the Format tab to give the title more style. Next, copy the pictures from the Title slide (Command+C) and paste into the new slide (Command+P) for design continuity.

13. Save your presentation (File > Save or Command+S).

14. Before delivering the presentation, use the spellcheck tool (Review > Spelling) to check for authority-undermining typing errors. Practise the presentation using the Play Presentation tool in the Slide Show tab.

15. Hook up to a HDTV or projector in your office conference room and select Presenter View from the Slide Show tab. Deliver your presentation using all of the tools mentioned back in Chapter two (*see* pages 81–82).

JARGON BUSTER

Action Button
A button where clicking or hovering the mouse over it triggers an Action, such as linking to a website or moving to the next slide.

Align
Control how text or an object appears within a slide, horizontally and vertically (e.g. hugging the left or right, or centre, top or bottom).

Animation
Effects that control how objects behave when entering and leaving a presentation (e.g. Fly, Fade, Float).

Arrange
Control the order in which objects appear within the slide by bringing them forward or sending them backwards.

Aspect Ratio
The height and width of slides relative to each other (e.g. 4:3 or 16:9).

AutoCorrect
When PowerPoint assumes you've made an error and corrects it.

AutoFormat
Makes automatic formatting changes to your presentation (e.g. 1/2 becomes ½).

Axis
The horizontal and vertical lines on which data is plotted (e.g. days of the week, ice cream sold).

Background Style
Controls the colours, shading, patterns or images that appear behind the objects on your slides.

Backstage View
Microsoft's pet name for the File tab, which controls most of the essential 'behind the scenes' functionality, such as saving, printing, etc.

Browser
A tool for viewing internet-based content (e.g. Internet Explorer, Firefox, Chrome).

Bullet
A text character that helps to arrange words in listed form.

Clip Art
Images, videos, illustrations and audio built into the PowerPoint software, which can easily be added to slides.

Clipboard
Stores information that users copy or cut from content placeholders or slides.

Content Placeholder
A design pre-set, which allows you to add objects like text, images, video and charts to a slide.

Crop
Trimming the size of an image.

Cursor
The icon that appears on the screen representing your mouse pointer.

Datasheet
The collection of figures from which a table or chart is created.

Default Settings
The pre-set actions that occur when accessing features within PowerPoint.

Demote
The action of moving a sentence or paragraph down one level within a list (the opposite of promote).

Drag
Selecting an object with your mouse, holding down the mouse button and pulling it to a new location.

Effects
Formatting tools that allow shadows, reflections, rotations and more.

Equations
A collection of numbers and symbols, usually representing a mathematical formula.

Excel
Microsoft Office spreadsheet program, useful in PowerPoint for creating charts.

Fill
The colour information within a shape. 'No fill' means that there's a clear background.

Fonts
The collective term for the different text styles.

Footers
Information that resides at the bottom of a slide (i.e. date, title, name).

Formatting
Altering the size, colour and style of an object in PowerPoint.

Grayscale
A slide, print-out or presentation which only features shades of grey.

Handout
A printed document which showcases each slide from your presentation.

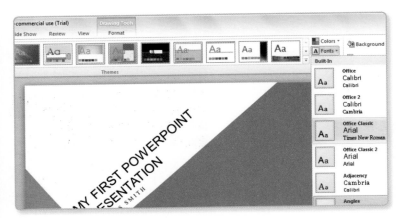

default formatting information for slides, handouts and notes. It can be customized, adjusted, added to and saved.

Merge
The process of combining two presentations to create one master document.

Motion Path
A custom animation feature, which allows an object to move across a pre-set path.

Object
Any item within PowerPoint (e.g. text box, photograph, shape, chart, table). Formatting and design tools can be applied to all objects.

Outline
Controls the colour of the text outline.

Pane
A vertical section of the PowerPoint Window (e.g. Slide View, Animation Pane, Current Slide View).

Header
Text information that appears at the top of one or all slides (usually features the title or date).

Hyperlink
A link to an object within a slide (e.g. a website, different presentation, next slide).

Justify
How text or an object sits within the placeholder. Text that is evenly spread across the text box, rather than aligned to the left, right or centre, is justified.

Landscape
A horizontally orientated

slide, presentation or handout.

Layouts
The differing slide designs available within a presentation (e.g. Title and Content, Blank, Two Content).

Legend
A table featuring a colour-coded key to categories represented within a chart.

Macros
Mini programs that allow users to repeat routine tasks automatically.

Master
A Master controls all of the

Portrait
A slide, handout or presentation with a vertical orientation.

Presentation
A collection of slides.

Promote
The action of moving a sentence or paragraph up one level within a list (the opposite of demote).

Quick Access Toolbar
Sitting above the Ribbon, it offers one-click access to a host of essential features.

Ribbon
The name for the PowerPoint user interface featuring tabs such as Home, Insert, Transitions.

Right-click
Hitting the button on the right side of your mouse. On Mac computers this is achieved by hitting Control+Click or, on newer models, by clicking the mouse button with two fingers.

Series
Information that appears within a data or chart. A series represents one group of data results.

Shapes
Types of objects that can be drawn on to slides.

SmartArt
Text-based diagrams which can represent a relationship, flow or hierarchy of information.

Start Button
The Windows icon in the bottom left corner of the screen: access PowerPoint and other programs from here.

Tab
Subsections of a Window, such as each of the options within the Ribbon (Home, Insert, Slide Show, etc.).

Theme
A combination of design features used throughout a presentation.

Trackpad
The touch-sensitive centre section on a laptop computer that acts like a mouse.

Transition
The means of moving between slides (e.g. Dissolve, Push, Wipe, Split).

WordArt
A text design feature that includes a host of colours, fills, outlines and effects.

FURTHER READING

ECDL Advanced Presentation Software Using Powerpoint 2016 (BCS ITQ Level 3), CiA Training, 2016.

Microsoft Official Academic Course: Microsoft PowerPoint 2013 MOS Exam 77-422, John Wiley & Sons, 2014.

Atkinson, Cliff, *Beyond Bullet Points 4th Edition: Using PowerPoint to tell a compelling story that gets results*, Microsoft Press, 2018.

Cox, Joyce and Lambert, Joan, *Microsoft PowerPoint 2013 Step By Step*, Microsoft Press, 2013.

Duarte, Nancy, *Resonate: Present Visual Stories That Transform Audiences*, John Wiley & Sons, 2010.

Duarte, Nancy, *slide:ology: The Art and Science of Creating Great Presentations*, O'Reilly Media, 2008.

Edney, Andrew, *PowerPoint 2007 in Easy Steps*, Computer Step, 2007.

Edney, Andrew, *PowerPoint 2010 in Easy Steps*, In Easy Steps Limited, 2010.

Edney, Andrew, *PowerPoint 2013 in Easy Steps*, In Easy Steps Limited, 2015.

Grover, Chris, *Office 2011 for Macintosh: The Missing Manual*, Pogue Press, 2010

Johnson, Steve, *Brilliant PowerPoint 2010:*
What You Need To Know and How You Do It, Prentice Hall, 2010.

Johnson, Steve, *Brilliant PowerPoint 2013: What You Need To Know and How You Do It*, Pearson Education Limited, 2013.

Kao, Wayne & Huang, Jeff, *Advanced Microsoft Office PowerPoint 2007: Insights and Advice From The Experts*, QUE, 2007.

LeVitus, Bob, *Office 2011 for Mac for Dummies*, John Wiley & Sons, 2011.

Lowe, Doug, *PowerPoint 2019 for Dummies*, John Wiley & Sons, 2018.

Lowe, Doug, *PowerPoint 2016 for Dummies*, John Wiley & Sons, 2015.

Lowe, Doug, *PowerPoint 2013 for Dummies*, John Wiley & Sons, 2013.

Lowe, Doug, *PowerPoint 2010 for Dummies*, John Wiley & Sons, 2010.

Reynolds, Garr, *Presentation Zen: Simple Ideas on Presentation Design and Delivery*, New Riders, 2011.

Roberts, David, *The Ultimate Guide to Visual Lectures*, David Roberts (Kindle edition), 2018.

Wempen, Faithe, *PowerPoint 2013 Bible*, John Wiley & Sons, 2013.

WEBSITES

www.actden.com/pp/
PowerPoint in the classroom.

www.dummies.com/software/microsoft-office/powerpoint/
The official online portal for the popular and entertaining *For Dummies* series of books, including a section on Microsoft Office and PowerPoint.

www.electricteacher.com/tutorial3.htm
Microsoft PowerPoint Tutorials.

www.lifewire.com/learn-how-presentations-4160663
Resources, tutorials, and tips for Microsoft PowerPoint and other presentation tools.

www.microsoft.com/en-gb/education
Microsoft Education's 'how to' pages.

www.microsoft.com/en-us/learning/exam-77-729.aspx
Take an exam in PowerPoint 2016.

www.msofficeforums.com/powerpoint/
A community-based resource for all Office products, including PowerPoint.

www.office.com
Get free trials of Microsoft Office, including PowerPoint, and access the vast knowledge base.

www.powerpointstyles.com/
Free PowerPoint templates for personal use.

www.presentationload.com/powerpoint
Premium pay-to-download PowerPoint template and slide designs.

www.presentationmagazine.com/
An online guide to making speeches and using PowerPoint. There are also free-to-download PowerPoint templates.

https://products.office.com/en-gb/compare-all-microsoft-office-products?tab=2
Office 365 Online Services – hosted in the Cloud.

www.sharepoint.com
Learn more about Sharepoint, Microsoft's business-centric collaboration tool.

https://support.office.com/en-ie/powerpoint
Microsoft's PowerPoint help page.

slideshop.com/powerpoint-templates/
A PowerPoint resource store featuring a host of templates, charts, shapes and diagrams.

https://templates.office.com/
Office Online templates.

INDEX

A

Access 16
Access Online 68
Action Buttons 190
  adding Action Buttons to
  slides 192–93
  types of Action 193
  types of Action Buttons
  191–92
adding charts 167
adding comments 203
adding equations 179–80
adding GIF files 152
adding hyperlinks 188–90
adding icons 139
adding images
  adding Clip Art 138–41
  adding pictures 136–38
  adjusting image's
  appearance 141–43
  adjusting style 144–45
  arranging text, images
  and objects 145–46
  creating custom photo
  album 147–48
  adding tables 160–64
adding text 58, 88–90
adding video and audio
  adding audio to
  presentation 154
  adding video 150–51
  adding video from
  sharing websites (PC
  only) 150
  audio 154
  on-slide media playback
  controls 156
  recording your own
  audio 155
  video and audio playback
  tools 156–59
animations 118
  adding GIF files 152–53

advanced animation and
  the Animation Pane
  123–25
Animation Painter 119
Animation Timings
  Pane 124
Animation Triggers (PC
  only) 123
Animations Tab 33
applying an
  animation 118
applying multiple
  animations 121
controlling duration of
  animation 125
Custom Path 121
delaying animation 125
Effect Options 122
Motion Path 120
reordering animations
  123–24
starting an
  animation 124
types of animation
  118–29
Apple Mac 9, 16
audio 26
  adding audio to
  presentation 154
  adding bookmark 157
  compatible audio file
  formats 155
  Media Size and
  Performance 198
  recording your own
  audio 155
  Trim Audio (PC only) 158
  video and audio playback
  tools 158–69
AutoCorrect 96–97
AutoFormat 97–98
AutoSave 42–43

B

background styles 52
  customizing 111–12
Backstage View 35–36, 67
  Close 36
  New 36
  Open 36
  Options 36
  Permissions 36, 197
  Prepare for sharing 35,
  197
  Print 36
  Properties 35
  Save 36
  Save as 36
birthday invitation 23
Blank Presentation 48, 55
broadcasting 77, 207
  broadcasting your
  presentation 209–11
  creating narration track
  207–08,
  delivering broadcast 211
  make a video 211–15
  starting web broadcast
  210–12
  using laser pointer 209
bullet points 58, 104–05
  adding new bullet point
  89
  AutoFormat 98
  customizing 105

C

calendars 23
CDs 205–206
Chart Tools 174
  adding titles, legends,
  labels and data tables
  172–73
  formatting chart
  elements 174
  PowerPoint chart analysis

  tools 173–74
  Shape Styles (PC) and
  Chart Styles (Mac) 171
charts 25
  adding charts 167
  Chart Tools layout tab
  171
  data 168
  types of chart 165–67
  working with Excel 167–
  74
classroom use 21
  re-creating history for
  teachers and students
  220–24
  teaching a film-making
  class 225–29
clickable slides 188
  Action Buttons 190–93
Clip Art 138
  adding Clip Art 138–41
clipboard 90
closing PowerPoint 42
  accidental closing and
  AutoSave 42–43
collaborating on
  presentation 194
  inviting comments 195
  saving your presentation
  online 199–200
  sending presentation via
  email 195
  sharing your presentation
  195–98
colours 52
  changing background
  colours 111–12
  changing font colours
  109–10
  changing theme colours
  110–11
  choosing font colours
  109–10

colour printing 71
making colour
    changes 143
More Colors 110
standard colours 110
WordArt and Text Styles
    112–14
comments 203–04
comparison tools 201–203
Compress Pictures 144
computers 72
    configuring to work on
        HDTV 74
    configuring to work with
        projector 74
content placeholders 60
    creating content
        placeholders 127
    deleting 91–92
    moving and resizing 126
Copy 90–91
coursework 21
cursor 34
Custom Slide Show 77
Cut 90–91
CVs 22

D
data 165
    adding data in Excel
        168–69
    data tables 173
    selecting, editing and
        refreshing data 170
default content slide 60
delivering presentation 81
    delivering broadcast 211
    drawing on slides 83
    starting presentation
        81–82
    using laser pointer 82
    using Presenter View
        83–85
Design Ideas 56, 137
design reminders 65
Draw tab 32
drawing on slides 83
drawing shapes 26, 181

adding style 183
customizing shapes 183
freeform shapes 184
types of shapes 181–83
DVDs 205
DVI (Digital Visual
    Interface) 73

E
editing text
    adding text 88–90
    Cut, Copy and
        Paste 90–91
    finding text within your
        presentation 93–94
    spellchecking your work
        94–100
    undoing mistakes 92
email 190
    sending presentation via
        email 195
equations 179–180
Excel 16, 167–69
    adding data in Excel
        168–69
    changing chart
        layout 171
    changing PowerPoint
        chart 169
    chart styles 171
    Chart Tools Design 169
    selecting, editing and
        refreshing data 170
    Switch Row/Column
        (Switch Plot on
        Mac) 170
external hard drives
    205–06

F
family budgeting/dieting
    22
    family diet and fitness
        regime 235–40
family trees 23
file extensions 38
    PDF (.pdf) 39
    PowerPoint Presentation

(.ppt, .pptx) 39
    saving to the cloud 39
    XPS (.xps, .xpsx) 39
flash drives 205–06
fonts 52
    changing font colours
        109–10
    changing fonts 106–07
    increasing and decreasing
        font size 102
    replacing fonts 108
    text fonts in themes
        107–08
footers 127
formatting text
    basic tools 106
    bullet points and
        numbered lists 104–05
    fonts 106–08
    increasing and decreasing
        font size 102
    text alignment 102–04
    text emphasis tools 101

G
GIF files 152
graphs 165

H
Handout Master 133
handouts 69, 127
HDMI (High Definition
    Multimedia Interface)
    73
HDTV (high definition
    television) 74
headers 127
help 11
home use 21–22
homework 21
hot tips 10–11
    Action Buttons 193
    add to Dictionary 96
    adding audio 154, 158
    adding video 151, 158
    adjusting images 141,
        142, 144, 146
    Align Text 104

animations 118, 122,
background colours 112,
beginning presentation
    76
changing spellchecker to
    UK English 100
clearing formatting 106
colour 142
Compress Pictures 144
copying, cutting and
    pasting text 91
creating narration
    track 208
deleting text 89
drawing shapes 182, 183
Excel 169
exiting File tab 37
finding PowerPoint on PC
    and Mac 15
fonts 108
hyperlinks 190
keeping display on
    screen 85
keeping PowerPoint
    within dock 28
keeping presentations
    simple 23
laser pointer 82
Mac Command key 41
making videos 213, 214
Master Slide layouts 131
Microphone 208
multiple presentations 32
naming and saving 38
numbered lists 105
Older Versions boxes 16
opening PowerPoint 27
Page Set-up 49
Pen tool 83
Photo Album 149
pictures 141, 142
Print settings 68
printing handouts 69
printing in colour 71
projectors 75
quizzes 26
Ribbon 30

saving your presentation online 199
selecting text 89
Slide Master 129, 130
SmartArt 25, 176
tables 163
templates 147
text size 102
themes 52
transitions 115, 117
underline options 102
Undo 92
undoing spellchecking 98
using comparison tools 202
video aspect ratio 214
WordArt 113, 114
hyperlinks 188
  hyperlink to computer file 189
  hyperlink to email address 190
  hyperlink to new document 189
  hyperlink to slide within presentation 189
  hyperlink to web page 189–90
  Mac command 188

I
Icons 139
image file formats 138
image rights 137
importing slides 216
  macros 217
  using slide libraries 217
information posts 22
iTunes 155, 188, 193

J
jargon buster 11, 246–49
job interviews 21
jokes 65

K
keyboard tools 81–82

L
labels 23, 172–73
Language 99–100
laptops 73, 74
laser pointer 82
lectures 21
legends 172
lyrics sheets 22

M
macros 217
media playback controls 156
memory sticks 205
Microsoft Office 15
  Office 365 18, 43, 44
  Office Presentation Service 210
Microphone 208
Models, 3D 139
Motion Path (PC)/Path Animations (Mac) 120
mouse tools 81–82

N
narration tracks 207–08
navigational tools 81–82
Notes 64–65
  increasing size of Notes Pane 65
  Notes Page View 65
Notes Master 132
numbered lists 104–05
  AutoFormat 97–98
  customizing 105

O
obtaining PowerPoint 43–44
office use 20–21
  office pitch 241–45
Office 365 18, 43, 44
  Autosave 43
  Office 365 vs. Office 2019 18–19
Office.com online templates 22, 56
OneDrive, saving to 40

OneNote 16, 96
opening presentation 40–41
Outline View 70
Outlook 16

P
passwords 35, 198
Paste 90–91
Path Animations (Mac)/ Motion Path (PC) 120
pen drives 205
Pen tool 83
photo albums 21, 147
  creating custom photo album 147–49
  family photo album 230–34
  images in templates 147–48
pictures 24
  adding artistic effects 143
  adding pictures 136
  adding pictures outside of content boxes 138
  adjusting size, repositioning and rotating 149–40
  aligning images or objects 146
  arranging text 145
  changing size using Format tab 140–41
  Compress Pictures 144
  grouping images or objects 146
  image file formats 138
  making colour changes 143
  making corrections 142
  Picture Border and Picture Effect 144
  Picture Layout and SmartArt 145
  Picture Style 144
  removing background 141–42

Reset or Change (PC only) 143
pitching ideas 20
planning trips 22
PowerPoint 8–11
  Backstage View 35–36
  changing size of PowerPoint Window 41–42
  classroom use 21
  closing PowerPoint 42–43
  cursor 34
  file extensions 38–39
  finding PowerPoint on PC and Mac 15
  future versions 19
  home use 21–22
  Microsoft Office 15–16
  obtaining PowerPoint 43–44
  office use 20–21
  Office.com online templates 22
  older versions 17–20, 25
  opening presentation 40–41
  PowerPoint Online 9–10
  PowerPoint Window 28–32
  presentation software 14
  Ribbon 32–33
  saving presentation 37–38
  saving as PowerPoint 97–2003 presentation 39
  slides 23–26
  starting PowerPoint on Mac 28
  starting PowerPoint on PC 27
PowerPoint Window 28–32
  Blank Presentation 48, 55
  changing size of PowerPoint Window 41–42
  Current Slide 29
  File tab 30

maximize 42
minimize 42
notes tab 31
Quick Access Toolbar
  (QAT) 30–31
restore down 42
Ribbon 29–30
scroll bars 32
Slide View 29
Status Bar 31–32
Presentation Changes 202
presentations
  adding new slide 60
  adding notes 64–65
  configuring page set-up
    and slide orientation
    49–50
  preparing to present
    72–80
  printing presentation
    66–71
  setting up your slide
    show 78–80
  showcasing your
    presentation 72–77
  slide layouts 61–63
  starting new
    presentation 48
  starting new
    presentation from
    themes and templates
    55–57
  starting to deliver
    presentation 81–83
  templates 53–54
  themes 51–53
  using Presenter View
    83–85
  writing slides 58–59
Presenter View 76, 83–84
  Presenter View window
    84–85
Print 36, 66
  printing on Mac 67
Print Preview 67
printing presentation 66
  collating print job 71
  multiple copies 68

print layout 69
print orientation 71
printing all or some
  slides 68
printing handouts 69
printing in Outline
  View 70
printing Notes Pages
  69–70
printing on Mac 67
printing using File tab
  (Backstage View) 67
saving to OneNote and
  Access Online 68
selecting printer 68
projectors 74
projects
  family diet and fitness
    regime 235–40
  family photo album
    230–34
  initiating a new policy
    244–47
  office pitch 241–45
  teaching a film-making
    class 225–29

Q
Quick Access Toolbar
  (QAT) 30
  customizing the QAT
    30–31
Quick Print 66

R
Redo tool 92
Reference Tools 99
Revisions pane 202
Ribbon 29–30
  additional tabs 33
  Animations 33
  Design 32
  Home 32
  Insert 32
  Review 33
  Slide Show 33
  Transitions 33
  View 33

S
sales reports 20
saving presentation 37–38
  saving new version
    37–38
  saving presentation
    online 199–200
  saving to OneDrive 39
scripts 65
scrolling 34
selecting
  images 139–40
  text 88–89
SharePoint 200
sharing your presentation
  194–98
  precautions before
    sharing 198
  SharePoint 200
shortcuts 10–11
showcasing presentation
  72–77
  computer or laptop
    screen 72
  HDMI 73
  HDTV 74
  mirroring presentation
    on two screens 75
  projectors 74
  selecting Presenter View
    76
  VGA & DVI 73
Sleep 85
Slide Changes 202
slide layouts 52, 61
  adding new layout to
    existing slide 61
  Blank 62
  Comparison 62
  Content with Caption 62
  Picture with Caption 62
  Section Header 62
  selecting layout when
    adding new slide 61
  Title 62
  Title and Content 61
  Two Content 62
slide libraries 216–17

slide masters 128–133
  adding another Slide
    Master 130–31
  adding recurring text
    and objects to master
    slide 130
  changing the Handout
    and Notes Masters 132
  creating new slide
    layouts 131–32
  editing Master Slide
    layouts 131–32
  editing Slide Master
    129–31
  saving Master Slides as
    Custom Template 132
  Slide Master View 128
  what's in a Slide Master?
    129
Slide Size button 49
Slide Show
  broadcasting 77
  Custom Slide Show 77
  Hide Slide 79
  Rehearse Timings 79
  Set Up Slide Show
    78–79
  starting from Current
    Slide 77
slides 23–26
  adding comments to
    slides 203–04
  adding headers and
    footers 127
  audio 26
  charts 25
  clickable slides 188,
    190–93
  creating content
    placeholders 127
  default content slide 60
  deleting slides 63
  drawing on slides 83
  duplicating slides 62
  importing slides 216–17
  moving and resizing
    content placeholders 126
  moving between slides 63

pictures 24
printing slides 68
rearranging slides 63
shapes and drawing 26
slide orientation 49
slide sizes 49–50
SmartArt 25
tables 25
text 24
transitions 26
videos 24
writing slides 58–59
SmartArt 25
  adding SmartArt
    diagram 176–78
  editing text 178
  finishing touches 178
  Picture Layout and
    SmartArt 145
  types of SmartArt
    175–76
Spellchecker 31, 95
spellchecking 94–96
  AutoCorrect 96–97
  completing spellcheck 96
  spellchecking as you
    type 94
  summoning Spelling
    tool 95
  using Spelling tool 95
Spotify 188
staff training 20
starting a new
    presentation 48
  configuring page
    set-up 49
  Mac 55
  selecting themes and
    templates 52–54
  slide orientation 49
  slide sizes 49–50
Status Bar 31–32
  Indicator 31
  Spellchecker 31
  Theme 31
  viewing options 31
  Zoom bar 32
subtitles 59

T
tables 25, 160–164
  adding style 162–63
  adding table 160–62
  editing table layout
    161–62
  populating a new
    table 164
templates 53–54
  Office.com online
    templates 22, 56
  saving Master Slides as
    Custom Template 132
  selecting 54
text 23
  adding new bullet
    point 89
  adding sub-points and
    multiple paragraph
    levels 90
  adding subtitle 59
  adding text to new
    content placeholder 59
  amending text 89
  arranging text, images
    and objects 145–46
  AutoCorrect 96–97
  AutoFormat 97–98
  Change Case 106
  Character Spacing 106
  choosing title 58
  copying text to
    clipboard 90
  correcting capitals 96
  cutting text 90–91
  deleting text 89, 91
  moving between text
    boxes 59
  find and replace 93–94
  finding text 93
  finding text on Mac 93
  increasing and
    decreasing font size 102
  languages other than
    English 99–100
  Line Spacing 106
  pasting text 91
  saving text 92

selecting section of text
    88–89
SmartArt 175–78
Strikethrough 106
text alignment 102–04
text direction 103–04
text effects 113–14
text emphasis tools 101
Text Fill 113
Text Shadow 114
Thesaurus tool 98–99
typing within text
    box 58
undoing mistakes 92
vertical text alignment
    103
Text Fill 113
Text Outline 113
themes 51–52
  background styles 52
  changing theme colours
    110–11
  colours 52
  fonts 52, 107–108
  selecting themes
    52–53, 55
  slide layouts 52
Thesaurus tool 98–99
titles 58, 62, 172–73
transitions 115–17
  adding transitions 116
  previewing transitions
    117
  transition options
    116–17
  types of transition
    115–16
Translate 99–100
transporting presentation
    205–06
  burn to CD or DVD 205
  external hard drive or
    memory stick 205–06

U
Undo tool 92
uploading your video to
    internet 214–15

V
version management
  Version History 38
VGA (Video Graphics
    Array) 73
videos 24, 207
  adding bookmark 157
  adding video 150–151
  adding video from
    sharing websites 150
  compatible video file
    formats 151
  creating narration track
    207–08
  creating video on
    Mac 212–13
  creating video on
    PC 214
  file formats 138,
    151, 155
  make a video 211–15
  Media Size and
    Performance 198
  Poster Frame 157
  Trim Video (PC
    only) 158
  uploading your video to
    internet 214–15
  using laser pointer 209
  video and audio
    playback tools 156–59
  video browser on
    Mac 151
  Video Tools Format
    tab 159
Vimeo.com 150

W
web broadcast 210–11
Windows
  Windows 7 17, 19
  Windows 8.1 16, 19
  Windows 10 17, 19, 27
Word 16

Y
YouTube.com 150,
    215, 222